Teach Us
To Pray

By J. W. ACKER

 CONCORDIA PUBLISHING HOUSE

SAINT LOUIS 18, MISSOURI

ACKNOWLEDGMENTS

Grateful acknowledgment is due the following publishers for permission to quote copyright material:

Book Mission of the E. L. C. for the poem "He Leadeth Me."

Harper & Brothers for the poem "Someone Had Prayed," from *The Lifted Lamp* by Grace Noll Crowell. Copyright 1942.

Moody Press for the poem "Prayer for the Home" by Martha Snell Nicholson.

Zondervan Publishing House for quotations from *Taking Hold of God* by Samuel M. Zwemer, D. D. Copyright 1936.

CONTENTS

I

Antiquity
and Universality of Prayer

PRAYER in the popular sense — an act by which man approaches his God — is undoubtedly the oldest and most universal of all religious rites. Prayer has played a prominent role in all religious systems. This observation led the German poet and philosopher Novalis to remark, "Prayer is to religion what thought is to philosophy."

Regardless of the truth or fallacy of this assertion, the conclusion seems to be obvious that the desire to pray is instinctive with man. As man's belief in the existence of the soul and in the reality of a hereafter seems to be innate, so there seems to be lodged in man's heart a natural impulse to pray. As naturally as the wing of the bird seeks flight or the fin of the fish takes to water, so the human heart yearns for a higher being, a god. Aware of his own utter helplessness, man instinctively seeks help from his god or gods, especially in times of adversity and distress. Some etymologists claim that the Greeks called man *anthropos* because he was a being with face upturned to God. Are we ever more natural than when facing God in prayer?

According to historical research the practice of prayer is exceedingly *ancient*. It is presumed to be older than magic; and some contend that it is more ancient than sacrifice itself, of which it may be the root. Very

5

primitive prayers, often expressed in terms of prevailing moral standards, are found in the ancient records of China, Egypt, Babylonia, India, Peru, and Mexico.

Sometimes these primitive prayers, usually addressed to the spirits of the forest or the sea or to the lesser gods, idols, and fetishes, are individual and spontaneous; sometimes they are collective and corporate, following some *ritual,* with or without the accompaniment of sacrifice.

But whatever the form of prayer among primitive races may have been, there can be no doubt that the act of prayer is a *universal* practice. Archaeological research indicates there has been no tribe of people, however degraded and barbarous, that has not prayed. Races have been discovered living without clothes, without houses, and without manufactures but never without some trace of prayer. Never did a traveler find a nation on the face of the earth which did not employ prayer in some form or other.

Not only does the Mohammedan prostrate himself in prayer at the call of the muezzin in the minaret; not only does the Buddhist worship three times a day over the relics of Buddha with flowers, perfume, and music; not only does the Confucianist perform ceremonial prostrations amid clouds of incense before the family shrine, whereon stand the wooden tablets of his ancestors — but among all races and in every religious system there are definite indications of the existence of prayer, even among the Negritos of the Philippine Islands, the Yamema of Tierra del Fuego, the Khonds of Orissa, India, and the Bushmen and Hottentots of South Africa. (A possible exception seems to be the Andamanese of Bengal Bay.)

Prayer among the ancient Greeks and Romans, consisting usually of short formulas supposed to possess magical power, was part of their public and private lives. Plato advises: "Every man of sense before beginning any important work will ask help of the gods." Plutarch reports that the great orator Pericles before making an address always prayed to the gods to bless his words. So also Seneca, the great Roman philosopher, has left records of his personal prayers.

Today also this natural impulse to pray should stir up the dull and apathetic spirits of men everywhere to address the Deity in prayer. Particularly should this be true of those who call themselves Christian, those who claim to know the only true God, the only real source of help and remedy for human ills. One would think that Christians, God's children, members of the household of God who have been called out of darkness into the marvelous light of God's revealed Word, stewards of the rich spiritual treasures of divine grace, would blush with shame when they compare their personal neglect of the blessings of true prayer with the futile clamor of the heathen for deliverance at the altars of their gods in the emergencies of life.

What is the reason that so many who otherwise seem to be genuine Christians do not practice the art of prayer as they should? Is it that materialism — the preoccupation with things that one can see, hear, smell, taste, and touch — has so warped their sense of values that they do not discern the need for this exercise of faith? Has their reliance on science and other human crutches led them away from leaning on God in prayer? Has the terrific pace that modern life sets for children of God so pre-empted their waking hours and exhausted their strength that they find little convenience and even

7

less mood for communion with their heavenly Father? Has family life become so disrupted today that it becomes increasingly difficult to assemble the members for meditation and prayer? Regardless of these or other reasons there is an admitted vacuum in this phase of Christian life. Perhaps a restudy of the need and power of prayer will help to remedy this deplorable situation.

II

DEFINITION

AND TERMINOLOGY OF PRAYER

PRAYER is of exceedingly great value to the Christian. Indeed, it is difficult to calculate the power or to overestimate the importance of true prayer in the life of a Christian. Witness this truism: The greater the number of fervent prayers spoken by Christians, the more abundant will be their blessings and the blessings of the congregations to which they belong; and again, the greater the number of praying Christian congregations, pastors, and teachers, the richer will be the increase in spirituality and the more abundant the services rendered to Christ, His kingdom, and the world at large.

Of course, to make such a sweeping assertion is not to equate prayer with a means of grace. Such are alone the divine Word and the holy sacraments. Nevertheless, effectual prayer is the *token*, the *evidence*, of faith and spiritual life bestowed through the agency of the means of grace. A Christian without prayer is like a body without a soul. He is a living spiritual corpse. Not without good reason, then, has prayer been variously likened to the thermometer or the pulse beat of the believer's spiritual life.

"By means of a certain stone, called a touchstone, in olden times people believed it was possible to determine whether a gem or a precious piece of jewelry was

genuine or not. The sham diamond might glitter ever
so brightly, the sham gold externally deceive the eye,
let the touchstone be applied, and its real character
would at once appear. Spiritually, in religion, there is
such a touchstone by which those who profess to serve
God can discover whether they are genuine Christians
or not, whether their religion is pure gold or inferior
metal, whether their faith is a gem of great price or
only worthless imitation, useless dross. That touchstone
of true spiritual life is prayer, communion with God,
for as a man communeth with his God, so he is." (Buchheimer, *Faith and Duty*, p. 156)

> Prayer is the soul's sincere desire,
> Uttered or unexpressed;
> The motion of a hidden fire
> That trembles in the breast.
>   — James Montgomery

If prayer is so vital to Christian faith and life, we
do well to inquire more fully into the true and exact
nature of effectual prayer. For this purpose a clear and
concise definition of prayer is desirable, even necessary.
Several fitting definitions may be supplied. One which
is eminently adequate and possesses all of the essential
requirements for God-pleasing prayer as set forth in
Holy Scripture is this: *Prayer is the communion of the
believing heart with the true God.*

This definition, moreover, is Scriptural, being based
on the dialog between the psalmist's heart and God.
In Psalm 27:8 David writes: "When Thou saidst, Seek
ye My face, my heart said unto Thee, Thy face, Lord,
will I seek." In response to the Lord's gracious invitation
"to seek His face" (or what is equivalent to that expres-

sion — "to commune with Him"), David's heart resolves to commune with the Lord, the true God of Israel. This he expects to do by prayer, for it is of prayer that the context speaks.

This view of prayer as a communion of the believer's heart by no means excludes the use of words in prayer. Rather they are the expression of the thoughts and meditation of the heart, even as David pleads, "Let the *words of my mouth* and the meditation of my heart be acceptable in Thy sight, O Lord, my Strength and my Redeemer" (Psalm 19:14). No cleavage between the communion of the heart and the utterances of the lips in the definition of prayer should be created, because for all ordinary purposes we may take for granted that the lips express the thoughts of the heart, even as our Savior declared, "Out of the abundance of the heart the mouth speaketh." (Matthew 12:34)

"All teachers of the Scriptures conclude that the essence and nature of prayer is nothing else than the elevation of the soul to, or the meditation of the heart on, God." (Luther, Erlangen edition, XXI, 166)

This definition of prayer as an act of spiritual communion on the part of the believer with the true God immediately suggests the thought that prayer is an *act of worship*. On this point all commentators, even those who are very radical in their treatment of the subject of prayer, apparently are agreed. From the fact that prayer is an act of worship are derived a number of conclusions regarding prayer that guide us in our prayer life. Hence the truism that prayer is an act of worship should be emphasized.

"After the preaching of the Gospel whereby God speaks to us, this is the greatest and foremost work, that by prayer we in turn speak to God." (Luther, Weimar edition, 46, 81)

As an act of worship, prayer must be addressed solely and alone to the one true God, "the Triune God, Father, Son, and Holy Spirit, three distinct persons in one divine essence." For Jesus says (speaking to the devil on the occasion of His temptation), "Thou shalt worship the Lord thy God, and Him only shalt thou serve" (Matthew 4:10). True prayer, prayer which alone avails before Him who answers before we call and hears while we are yet speaking, is therefore the prayer which is made to the one true God as He has revealed Himself in Scripture.

Prayers made to any other are so much wasted effort and time. Prayers addressed to man-made idols of wood, stone, bronze, silver, and gold, prayers made to the saints in an effort to enlist them as intermediaries for us, prayers directed to figments of man's imagination, such as the "Supreme Ruler of the Universe," the "Supreme Being of the Universe," and the "Exalted Ruler of the Universe" of lodges, or prayers lifted up to false gods, as by Jews, Mohammedans, Hindus, Unitarians, theosophists, Christian Scientists, etc., merely are showered on lifeless or nonexistent beings and fall on deaf ears. Writes the Psalmist: "Our God is in the heavens; He hath done whatsoever He hath pleased. Their idols are silver and gold, the work of men's hands" (Psalm 115:3-4). All prayers to such idols of man's creation have as their reward the silence of futility and the dull vacuum of hope.

It is strange how men who are otherwise conservative in their views of prayer fail to grasp this fundamental fact that the only effectual prayer is the prayer addressed to the God of the Bible. We find, for instance, that Samuel M. Zwemer in his *Taking Hold of God* — in many respects a very readable and Scripturally sound treatment of the subject of prayer — strives in his sympathy for the benighted heathen to discover some worth in their prayer and to imagine some divine blessing resting upon their plea for help. He writes (p. 95):

"Surely He who hears the young ravens when they cry hearkens to the voice of these children in the dark. He that planted the ear, shall He not hear? He that formed the eye, shall He not see? He that chastiseth the heathen, shall He not correct? He that teacheth man knowledge, shall He not know?"

However great our sympathy for the poor, ignorant, and confused heathen, we must not permit the loving impulses of our heart to obscure the clear light the Word of God sheds on this controverted point. The Scriptures condemn the prayer of the heathen as an utterly valueless act, as void of all spiritual significance as the meaningless gibberish of the mentally deranged inmate of an asylum for the insane. Remarks Alexander Maclaren: "Heathenism has no true prayer. Wild cries and passionate desires flung upward to an unloved God are not prayer; and that solace and anchor of the troubled soul is wanting in all the dreary lands given to idolatry."

The Scriptural requirement that prayer be addressed to the one true God clearly implies that only a Christian can pray in a manner acceptable to God, for the Christian alone knows who the true God is and instinctively turns to Him in time of need. This St. Paul teaches in no uncertain manner when he writes to the Romans (15:13, 14): "For whosoever shall call upon the name of the Lord shall be saved. How then shall they call on Him in whom they have not believed? And how shall they believe in Him of whom they have not heard?" This Word of God in sweeping fashion excludes from the rightful use of prayer all those who are not Christians. Hence our definition of prayer includes the phrase "of the believing heart" as a necessary element of prayer.

Concerning the necessity of true faith in prayer Luther writes (St. Louis VIII, 361 ff., in J. T. Mueller, *Christian Dogmatics,* p. 431): "Before we become Christians and believe, we do not know what and how we should pray. Although a person prays ever so earnestly [viewed externally], yet [before conversion] the Spirit of grace is not there. . . . There is [then] no faith in divine grace and mercy for Christ's sake, and the heart always remains uncertain, so that it must ever doubt whether it is heard; it deals with God only on the ground of its own holiness or that of others, without Christ, as if God should humble Himself before it and be prevailed upon to bestow His grace or help for our sake and thus become our servant or debtor. To do this means not to merit grace, but wrath; it is not a prayer, but rather a mockery of God."

A Christian enjoys a most blessed relationship with the Triune God. The Bible describes this close relationship as that of a spiritual Father to spiritual children, a relationship in which true believers are at all times privileged, yes, even urged to address Him lovingly and devotedly as they do in the Lord's Prayer, "Our Father." In his explanation of these words of the Lord's Prayer, Luther makes the following appropriate and familiar remarks concerning this relationship between the believing Christian and the Lord of the heavens:

14

"God would by these words tenderly invite us to believe that He is our true Father and that we are His true children, so that we may with all boldness and confidence ask Him as dear children ask their dear father."

This is precisely the spirit which St. Paul would implant and cultivate in our hearts when he writes to the Romans (8:15): "Ye have not received the spirit of bondage again to fear; but ye have received the Spirit of adoption, whereby we cry, Abba, Father." And again to the Galatians (4:6, 7): "Because ye are sons, God hath sent forth the Spirit of His Son into your hearts, crying, Abba, Father. Wherefore thou art no more a servant but a son; and if a son, then an heir of God through Christ." Christians, as the true spiritual children of God, are at all times heirs in and through Christ of all the treasures of heaven.

Caspari relates this story: "Themistocles, who rebuilt the city of Athens, once was sent into exile by his fellow citizens. Not knowing whither to turn for shelter, he fled to King Admetus, his outspoken enemy. Fearing death from the king's hands, Themistocles, on arriving in the hall of the king's palace, took the king's little son into his arms, approached the king, and said, 'Dear king, in the name of your son, whom I know you love, I ask for mercy.' At the sight of his son the king was so deeply moved that he forgave Themistocles and received him into his home. In the same manner we, who have offended God by our many sins, must bring Jesus, His Son, our Savior, to Him in our prayers and for His sake ask Him to forgive us our sins. Then God will not only pardon us but will also prove Himself to be our true and genuine Father." (Quoted in *Concordia Pulpit*, VII, 313)

In this conviction we confidently and courageously approach the throne of grace with our prayers, ever mindful that He who has sent "the Spirit of His Son into our hearts" to cry, "Abba, Father," will also without fail incline a favorable ear to us and answer our prayer according to His promises and good pleasure. Luther remarks in this connection: "Behold, now, how a father acts toward his child, and again the child toward the father. Even though the father be not natural, nevertheless the name [of father] inspires such a sincere and comforting confidence that one looks [confidently] to Him for all blessings. . . . For that purpose St. Paul desires to instruct us . . . with such natural confidence to experience what sort of Father God is and what we are to look for from Him." (St. Louis XII, 878, 879)

Such a tone of confidence in prayer is the product of the true saving faith alone. Without faith in Christ there can be no such assurance in our heart that God as our true Father regards our prayer with favor. Without faith, disturbing doubt and distressing fear must terrorize the heart. God can be nothing else than a wrath-filled judge and a consuming fire for him who does not believe that he is reconciled to God by the death of His Son.

Contrast the panic-stricken state of mind and heart of the unbeliever with the filial confidence which inspires the believing Christian. The believer knows that he is a child of God by virtue of his adoption that has taken place in Christ, and he can approach and petition the Lord of Glory as a kind and loving Father. How comforting it must be for all Christians in the hour of distress to hear or read these soothing words of Paul to the Galatians (3:26): "Ye are all the children of God by faith in Christ Jesus."

16

Surely these words must dispel the gloom of despair, put to rout all raging doubts, and inspire us with a heaven-born confidence to make use of the privileges of our spiritual heritage as children of God through faith in Christ to come before His throne of grace in prayer to receive satisfaction for all our wants. Such confident exercise of our privileges as children of God must and will follow upon the dawning in our hearts of the consciousness of this filial relationship with our heavenly Father as a gift of faith in Christ.

The unconverted man cannot possess such a confident attitude toward God, for he is spiritually "dead in trespasses and sins." The ability to pray as God would have us pray is the gift of the Holy Spirit, which He bestows on us through the means of grace, the Word and the sacraments. Does not the apostle declare in Galatians 4:6: "God hath sent forth the Spirit of His Son into your hearts, crying, Abba, Father," and again, Romans 8:15, 16: "The Spirit of adoption, whereby we cry, Abba, Father . . . itself beareth witness with our spirit that we are the children of God"? Accordingly, it is God's Spirit who prompts us in every good work, who teaches us with childlike confidence to cry to God, "Abba, Father," and impels us to express this confidence in God-pleasing prayer.

If we feel ourselves incapable of or disinclined to prayer, it is that selfsame Spirit of God who conquers our spiritual infirmities and expels the sinful coldness, as St. Paul testifies, Romans 8:26, 27: "Likewise, the Spirit also helpeth our infirmities; for we know not what we should pray for as we ought; but the Spirit itself maketh intercession for us with groanings which cannot be uttered. And He that searcheth the hearts knoweth what is the mind of the Spirit, because He

17

maketh intercession for the saints according to the will of God." From this passage it becomes obvious that the Spirit, and He alone, confers all validity and power on the prayers of the saints or believers, for whom "He maketh intercession."

In this vein Luther also writes: "When the Holy Spirit comes and quickens the hearts with the right confidence in God's goodness and mercy through Christ, then it follows that one will be able to pray properly and will become eager and willing thereto. But without this Spirit all prayer is impossible." (St. Louis XIII, 609)

Spurgeon similarly comments: "A true prayer is the autograph of the Holy Ghost upon the renewed heart."

Finally, the prophet Zechariah also alludes to the Holy Spirit as the Spirit of prayer when he calls Him "the Spirit of grace and of supplications." (Zechariah 12:10)

Briefly, then, our definition of prayer as "communion of the believing heart with the true God" implies that true prayer is an act of worship confidently addressed to the Triune God as the Christian's heavenly Father through faith in Christ Jesus, generated by the Holy Spirit through the means of grace.

It is surpassingly strange that any author who presumes to write on this subject should attempt with any trace of Scriptural sanction to classify as valid prayer the pagan plea to some higher power for help. When, therefore, we or others refer to the prayers of the unconverted, this does not mean that according to Scriptural standards such prayers are acceptable in the sight of God. Rather, because such prayers lack faith as their foundation and childlike confidence as their spirit, both of which are distinct gifts of the Holy Spirit, they do

18

not constitute actual prayer but are an abomination and a mockery before God.

Another erroneous view of prayer is to regard it as a means of grace. Calvinists, synergists, and Arminians urge the alarmed sinner to search for assurance of salvation in prayer. Revivalists throughout the length and breadth of our land today advise those who are still unconverted to plead, to struggle, and to wrestle with God in prayer until they have found the faith. But as we have repeatedly observed, the unconverted, the unbeliever, does not pray. Only the Christian actually prays when prayers are made. Prayer, therefore, is not a *means of grace* by which we may first obtain faith but rather a *fruit* of living faith already bestowed by the Spirit of God through the means of grace. To regard prayer as a meritorious means by which grace and salvation are secured is often a fatal error, for in many instances it leads to partial or total rejection of the Gospel of Christ.

Before proceeding further with the nature of prayer it might be beneficial to glance briefly at the terminology sometimes employed in prayer. In Holy Scripture a number of terms directly referring to the subject of prayer are mentioned. Thus Philippians 4:6 employs four expressions: "Be careful for nothing; but in everything by *prayer* and *supplication* with *thanksgiving* let your *requests* be made known unto God."

Luther explains these terms as follows: "Prayer is nothing else than the words of conversation [prayer in general], as, for instance, the Lord's Prayer, the Psalms, and the like, in which at times something else is said alongside of that for which we pray." Of supplication he remarks: "Supplication means to agitate or reinforce prayer by means of something else, as when I petition

19

a man through the agency of his father's will, or for the sake of something which he cherishes or values highly. Thus when we pray God through His Son, by the intercession of His saints, on account of His promises, or because of His name." He defines requests as follows: "Requests are when one mentions those things which weigh upon oneself and on account of which one prays in prayer and supplication; as, for instance, in the Lord's Prayer there is to be found a prayer and seven requests [petitions]." Concerning thanksgiving he says: "Thanksgiving is to narrate benefits received in order thereby to strengthen our confidence that we may expect an answer for the things for which we pray." (St. Louis XII, 94)

It will suffice to mention one more Bible passage in which several terms relating to prayer are grouped, 1 Timothy 2:1, where the apostle admonishes his understudy Timothy: "I exhort therefore that, first of all, *supplications, prayers, intercessions,* and *giving of thanks* be made for all men." Beyond those which have already been explained in the citation from Luther, only one new term here appears: "intercession," which denotes a petition made in behalf of someone else. Intercessory prayer is also an important phase of prayer, for we are not merely to direct requests to the Lord solely for ourselves, but we should in our daily prayers also include petitions for the welfare of others.

Among other expressions in the Bible that signify prayer are the following: "call," "call upon," "call upon the name," "ask," "seek," "seek the face," "knock," "visit" (Isaiah 26:16), "meditation of heart," etc., all of which are self-explanatory. It would contribute little to our purposes to enumerate the entire list or to describe the glorious variety of expressions which appear upon the pages of that holy volume in speaking of prayer.

It can readily be understood that theologians, confronted with such an abundance and variety of terms for prayer in Holy Writ, have attempted different classifications of prayers.

Thus Luther in his explanation of the Second Commandment divides prayer into three groups: *prayer, praise,* and *thanksgiving.* Divided in this manner, prayer represents petition; praise signifies the exposition and glorification of God's attributes, such as His omnipotence, love, kindness, and mercy; while thanksgiving denotes the recognition in thoughts, words, and deeds of blessings received by us.

Again, in his exposition of Philippians 4:6, Luther reaches a fourfold division of prayer resulting in *prayer, supplication, thanksgiving,* and *request, or petition,* with the distinction mentioned previously. Others speak of a threefold classification of all prayers into supplications, intercessions, and thanksgiving.

For the sake of clarity the simple, familiar, and logical division of prayer into the two parts of *petition* and *thanksgiving* is probably preferable. Franz Pieper, in his *Christliche Dogmatik* (III, 95), tersely remarks that this division suffices. This is the division which we ordinarily make in our own minds and which is generally employed in discussions of prayer.

If this last-mentioned twofold classification be observed, petitions would include intercessions. The petitions we address to the Giver of all good things may readily comprehend the prayers which are made for our fellow men. In fact, the latter, aside from any logical or technical considerations, should automatically be included with the requests made for self. Similarly, the distinction between praise and thanksgiving is ordinarily obscured in the average lay mind, so that for general purposes these closely related concepts may well be grouped together under the caption of thanksgiving.

Authors usually distinguish five elements in the construction of a prayer: (1) adoration, (2) thanksgiving, (3) confession, (4) petition, and (5) intercession. These five parts constitute the well-rounded prayer. When these ingredients are all present, the Christian may be certain that he has overlooked no essential in the mechanics of praying. In this analysis of the ideal prayer the only terms not previously defined are adoration and confession. Adoration is nothing other than the recital of the attributes and virtues of Deity, while confession embraces all the outpourings of a penitent heart.

In all attempts to define and classify prayer one note of warning should be sounded. Beware of making prayer a pretty piece of rhetoric, lest the temptation to analyze and to synthesize our oral communications with God so complicate the process as to impede the freedom and spontaneity of our prayers.

III

THE BASIC PRINCIPLES OF PRAYER

HAVING somewhat familiarized ourselves with the definition, terms, and general divisions of prayer, we are prepared to approach the subject of the manner in which prayers should be made. And by this we do not mean the physical bearing of the suppliant in prayer but rather the spiritual manner of the presentation of his petition. In this connection we are not concerned with the externals but rather with the sentiment of prayer which bespeaks a disposition of the heart.

Although the urge to pray is instinctive with man, the art of praying must be learned. The man who wishes to pray properly must enter the school of prayer, in which we are all pupils till our dying day and where there is but one Schoolmaster, He whom the disciples besought, "Lord, teach us to pray."

The Lord has in Holy Scripture prescribed the fundamental requirements of His course in the school of prayer. From this source book of divine revelation we learn that the first basic principle of prayer is that it must be made *in harmony with the will of God*.

St. John writes regarding this point: "This is the confidence that we have in Him, that, if we ask anything *according to His will*, He heareth us" (1 John 5:14). Jesus Himself set the perfect pattern of subordinating His will to the will of God when in the Garden of Gethsemane, wrestling with the crushing burden of the sins of the world, the perspiration trickling in droplets of blood from His lordly brow, He implored His heavenly Father to remove "the cup" of suffering from Him but quickly added, "nevertheless, not My will but Thine be done" (Luke 22:42). Moreover, in that prayer of prayers, the Lord's Prayer, our Savior taught us to pray in keeping with God's will, "Thy will be done on earth as it is in heaven."

Certainly, if we are at all intelligent beings, we must recognize the sovereignty of God in all things. We are God's creation. His supporting hand preserves us. He has redeemed us by the blood of His beloved Son. Therefore we belong to Him body and soul. We are under every moral obligation to obey and serve Him. Yet He would not have us be as bound slaves but as servants who cheerfully do His will. His will is that we be His instruments to discharge His purposes concerning us and the world in which we live. Our prayers to Him must ever, therefore, reflect His will.

We stand in relation to God, who in Christ is our heavenly Father, as children to their earthly parents. It would be stupid for children to dictate to their parents, for such action implies that children feel they know more than their parents. What is worse, it would be presumptuous for children to impose their will on their parents, for such conduct breathes an insolence born of ingratitude. Similarly our prayers to the Almighty must never take the form of dictation or even advice, for we must ever acknowledge His superior wisdom and trust His unquestioned love. The spirit of our petitions must always be: "God's will be done."

Prayer, by inference then, *is not so much to ask what we wish of God as to ask what God wishes of us.* Alexander Maclaren, the great Scot divine, put it this way: "Christ loves us a great deal too well to give our foolish and selfish wills the keys of His treasure-house. The condition of our getting what we will is our willing what He desires."

The next indispensable factor in prayer is that it must be made *in Jesus' name*. The Savior sets forth this requirement in John 16:23: "I say unto you, Whatsoever ye shall ask the Father *in My name*, He will give it you." This condition, that we must approach the Father in prayer in Jesus' name, is so important because without Christ our sins would make us "children of wrath, even as others." Apart from Christ, God is a consuming fire, effectually barring the approach of any self-satisfied sinner. But in and through Christ as our only Mediator and Advocate, He is a tender, loving Father, who at all times invites our approach in prayer.

The apostle Paul writes, 1 Timothy 2:5, 6: "There is one God, and one Mediator between God and men, the man Christ Jesus, who gave Himself a ransom for all." This all-sufficient and all-atoning ransom, which our Savior Jesus Christ paid on the cross with His holy, precious blood as of a Lamb without blemish and without spot, provides free and unhindered access for us to the throne of the righteous God, as the apostle declares, Ephesians 2:18: "For through Him [Christ] we . . . have access by one Spirit unto the Father."

Hence, to pray in Jesus' name is, in effect, to pray relying not on our righteousness and merit but with full and firm confidence in Christ as our meritorious Redeemer as well as only Mediator and Advocate. In this spirit the saints of all times have prayed.

Even in the *Old Testament times,* when one would not expect the recognition of this requirement of prayer to be so fully developed in God's people, examples

25

abound of those who sensed their own unworthiness to pray but who notwithstanding appealed to the Lord in prayer trusting in the mercy of a God whose wrath over sin was appeased by an atonement to be accomplished at the hands of the promised Savior.

Such reliance of the men of God in the Old Testament dispensation upon the Messiah's promised reconciliation of men with God is clearly manifested in Daniel's prayer (9:18): "We do not present our supplications before Thee for *our* righteousnesses but for *Thy* great mercies." He visualized God as merciful to mankind through the perfect satisfaction of the Christ to come.

So also Jeremiah in prayer throws himself upon the Lord's tender mercy, which was made possible by the satisfaction to be rendered by the Messiah to come, when he says (14:7): "O Lord, though our iniquities testify against us, do Thou it *for Thy name's sake;* for our backslidings are many; we have sinned against Thee." Abjectly prostrating himself before the Lord, he pleads his sinfulness and for forgiveness appeals to God's love in the Christ to come.

And now a few New Testament examples will suffice to convince us that the children of God living in the days of prophecy fulfilled found refuge in Christ by prayer. The Book of Acts indicates that when the early Christians prayed, they confided solely and alone in the merits of Jesus Christ, whom they preached, whom they confessed, and for whom they suffered martyrdom.

How completely their confidence centered in Christ is illustrated by the circumstances at Stephen's stoning. Acts 7:59, 60 reads: "And they stoned Stephen calling upon God and saying, Lord Jesus, receive my spirit. And he kneeled down and cried with a loud voice,

Lord, lay not this sin to their charge. And when he had said this, he fell asleep." Twice in the hour of death, according to the divine record, he prays to Jesus' name. And as he did, so did also the rest of the holy people of his day, for whom he is merely an illustrious example. Likewise down through the ages it has been the pious practice of the Christian fathers to present their petitions privately and publicly in Jesus' name.

Accordingly, we Christians observe the commendable custom of commencing or closing our prayers with such expressions as "in Jesus' name," "for Jesus' sake," "for Christ's sake," "through Jesus Christ, our Lord," etc., to indicate that our prayers are presented through Christ as our Mediator and Advocate and trusting in His meritorious satisfaction. The name of Jesus is that golden key that opens the Father's heart and gives access to the treasures which "eye hath not seen nor ear heard neither have entered into the heart of man."

However, lest this subject of prayer in Jesus' name be somewhat misunderstood, it should be noted in passing that it is not necessary always to employ precisely this expression "in Jesus' name" or some equivalent in prayer. That or some similar phrase is implied when prayer is lifted to the throne of grace in complete reliance of the heart upon the redemption accomplished by Christ. However, since public prayer acts as a confession of faith, the expression "in Jesus' name" should at all times be included in prayers publicly made.

And yet another brief remark in this connection. Prayer made in Jesus' name has as a corollary: Prayer must be made *in a humble spirit*. He who actually reposes his confidence in the redemptive work of Christ must first have recognized his own sinfulness and consequent unworthiness in the sight of God. Granted

27

that the earnestly praying Christian realizes his desperate spiritual condition before God, how can he be other than humble when praying?

The familiar parable of the Pharisee and the Publican is intended to convey the truth that humble prayer alone avails before God. The Pharisee, who, puffed up with his own conceit and radiating smug self-satisfaction, thanks God that he is not as other men are, is rejected; whereas the publican, overwhelmed by the sense of his guilt, smites upon his breast and humbly begs, "God, be merciful to me, a sinner," and is accepted by God. Christ concludes this parable with the significant observation: "Everyone that exalteth himself shall be abased; and he that humbleth himself shall be exalted." (Luke 18:14)

Intimately connected with the subject of prayer in Jesus' name is prayer with *firm confidence*. Confidence is also a vital factor of Christian prayer. By confidence in this connection is meant not so much Christian faith in general in the Savior and His atoning work, as faith, unwavering and unhesitating reliance, in the promises of Scripture concerning the power of and answer to prayer. Such confidence is the product alone of the Holy Spirit working on the human heart through the agency of the Gospel promises. (The place of general Christian faith in valid prayer has already been described. Here the importance of unremitting confidence in the Scriptural assurances of answered prayer shall engage our attention.)

Confidence in God's promises that prayer will be answered is required by our Savior Himself as an important element of the God-pleasing prayer when He promises: "All things whatsoever ye shall ask in prayer, *believing*, ye shall receive" (Matthew 21:22). What a glorious promise is herewith presented to all Christians! The force of this expression "all things whatsoever" should in no wise be emasculated or circumscribed; for, since the will of the praying believer should coincide with the good and gracious will of the Triune God, he will request only those things which it is God's will to give him, and hence truly "all things whatsoever" he will ask in prayer will actually be his portion, provided only that he believes, has confidence in the promises of the Lord, is persuaded that the Lord is able and willing to execute His promises.

When the father of the epileptic child brought his son to the Savior to be healed of the evil spirit, Jesus admonished the father: "If thou canst believe, all things are possible to him that believeth" (Mark 9:23). And thus it is ever. The Lord demands faith in Him and His promises, confidence in His power and determination to grant the desires of the Christian heart. "Our prayers are to remind God. The truest prayer is that which bases itself on God's uttered will. The prayer that prevails is a reflected promise. Our office in prayer is but to receive on our hearts the bright rays of His Word and to flash them back like a mirror to heaven from whence they came" (Alexander Maclaren). The prayer that commences with confidence and endures with patience will end in thankfulness, triumph, and praise.

The opposite of confidence in prayer is doubt. Doubt is akin to unbelief. As firm confidence in Christ, His promises, His omnipotent power, His loving-kindness, and His unchanging truthfulness is true saving faith viewed from a certain angle, or faith active in a certain field of operation, so doubt is a type of unbelief.

29

Doubt in prayer is positively condemned, both by word and example, in Holy Scripture. Thus writes, for instance, James (1:5-7): "If any of you lack wisdom, let him ask of God, that giveth to all men liberally and upbraideth not; and it shall be given him. But let him ask in faith, nothing wavering. For he that wavereth is like a wave of the sea driven with the wind and tossed. For let not that man think that he shall receive anything of the Lord." Again, Paul commands, 1 Timothy 2:8, "I will therefore that men pray everywhere, lifting up holy hands, without wrath and *doubting*." These passages clearly denounce doubting prayer as vain and unavailing. The Lord will by no means tolerate doubt in prayer.

Whoever therefore prays filled with doubts relating to the efficacy of his prayer or the probability of God's answer only succeeds in defeating the purpose of prayer and in insulting the merciful and omnipotent Lord. Luther says: "A prayer that rises from a heart trembling with doubt gets nothing from God. You do not pour anything into a vessel that is being moved and jerked about." A prayer which proceeds from a heart beclouded with doubt is sheer mockery, a sinful monstrosity in the sight of God.

Another important factor of Christian prayer is *fervency*. True prayer is at all times fervent. The fervent prayer inherits a glorious promise, a promise written by the inspired pen of James (5:16): "The effectual fervent prayer of a righteous man availeth much." The fervent prayer also has an illustrious example in Christ, our Savior. We need but think of Him in the Garden of Gethsemane when His prayers culminated in that agony of fervency which produced beads of crimson perspiration that trickled down His wan countenance, or of the

30

description given of the Master's prayers in Hebrews 5:7: "Who [Christ] in the days of His flesh, when He had offered up prayers and supplications with strong crying and tears unto Him that was able to save Him from death and was heard in that He feared." From these facts we gather that, to avail much before God, prayer must be fervent.

"Prayer without fervency is no prayer; it is speaking, not praying. Lifeless prayer is no more prayer than the picture of a man is a man." (Richard Watson)

Incense can neither smell nor ascend without fire; no more does prayer unless it arises from spiritual warmth and fervency. A prayer coming from a spiritually cold and indifferent heart, like cold air, does not rise to heaven. Fervency of prayer usually bespeaks a believing heart, although it is true that the heathen and all those in the visible Christian church who reject the vicarious atonement of Christ also pray with a certain earnestness and devotion. In their instance, however, such religious emotions flow from the flesh and not from true faith. The devil, who "worketh in the children of disobedience," can simulate the external characteristics of Christian prayer in those who are still "dead in trespasses and sins."

If prayer must be truly fervent to be effectual, then it follows that prayer dare never be a mere babbling or vain repetition of words. "When ye pray *use not vain repetitions,* as the heathen do; for they think that they shall be heard for their much speaking," warns the Savior (Matthew 6:7). Such thoughtless prattle occurs when parishioners monotonously thumb their rosaries or race through their Pater Nosters and Ave Marias with machine-gun rapidity.

Even among those who would undertake their prayers in a spirit of devotion and utmost fervency, carelessness and thoughtlessness in prayer at times becomes a disturbing factor because of the many distractions of our worldly-minded flesh. During prayer the mind of the Christian, which despite its renewal wrought by God's Holy Spirit is nevertheless still afflicted with the infirmities of the flesh, often plays the part of the truant lad who slips away from school to play marbles or to go fishing with his cronies.

Luther remarks appropriately anent the recitation of the Lord's Prayer: "The Lord's Prayer is the greatest martyr on earth. It is a pity above all pities that such a prayer by such a Master should be so terribly abused in all the earth. Many pray the Lord's Prayer a thousand times a year, and though they prayed it a thousand years, yet they have not properly prayed one letter thereof." And again he censures thoughtlessness in the Lord's Prayer: "They who merely recite the words of the Lord's Prayer without praying them with their heart are like a book which reproduces the thoughts of another but itself is without any understanding; such people are like the pipes of an organ which play a beautiful melody but lack all appreciation."

Only the prayer which is thoughtful, earnest, and fervent avails much. We must always have our thoughts riveted on the subject of our petition. That is the only sort of prayer which has any promise of answer. Cold, lifeless, and idle prayers are like birds without wings, like arrows without feathers. (As acts of worship such prayers are surpassed even by the parrots with their meaningless chatter.) How can we ever expect God to be present in our prayers to bless them if we ourselves are absent with our hearts from them? Obviously, mere lip prayers are lost prayers.

Also all prayers proceeding from an unforgiving heart are not heard. This is clear from such a passage as Mark 11:25, 26: "When ye stand praying, forgive if ye have aught against any, that your Father also which is in heaven may forgive you your trespasses. *But if ye do not forgive, neither will your Father which is in heaven forgive your trespasses.*" Again, here also applies that familiar and oft-quoted advice of the Savior, Matthew 5:23, 24: "Therefore, if thou bring thy gift to the altar and there rememberest that thy brother hath aught against thee, leave there thy gift before the altar, and go thy way; first be reconciled to thy brother, and then come and offer thy gift."

How can we ever hope to receive a blessing at the altar of prayer if we are not first reconciled to our brother? And yet, how often do not only the rank and file of church members but even those who take a prominent part in the work of the church fail to grasp that, when they utter the words of the Fifth Petition of the Lord's Prayer, they are actually promising to forgive all offenses, imagined or real, which they have suffered at the hands of their fellow men.

The ignorance of many Christians concerning the actual portent of the promise they make each time they recite the Lord's Prayer, yea, rather their *refusal to adjust the standards of their lives* to the requirements of this petition, is simply appalling. They fail to realize that the petition for pardon of our sins dies on our lips unless for His sake who died for us and rose again *"we forgive those who trespass against us."* To amend our prayers in this respect we need first by the grace of God to learn the lesson of love for all humanity.

33

For if we love not our brother, whom we have seen, how can we say we love God, whom we have not seen? (1 John 4:20)

Finally, to meet the requirements of Holy Scripture, our textbook in the school of prayer, prayer must be made "in spirit and in truth." This Christ expects of us according to John 4:24: "God is a Spirit; and they that worship Him must worship Him *in spirit and in truth.*"

As the context reveals, these words refer to the ceremonial practices current among the Israelites, according to which certain times, certain places, and certain rituals in worship were prescribed. With the passage of time, however, prayer became a mere outward formality among the Jews, who insisted on the exact observance of all details of the ritual of prayer but neglected to stress the importance of the chief part of prayer, the communion of the heart with the Triune God. In this passage the Lord condemns such spiritless superficiality in prayer.

The phrase "in spirit and in truth" implies that prayer should proceed from a fervent inner impulse without any dependence on particular customs and practices, which have only symbolical value. The expression "in spirit" *(en pneumati)* contrasts with mere externality in prayer, while the words "in truth" *(en aletheia)* are diametrically opposed to the overemphasis on the symbolism of the Jewish ceremonies.

Jesus does not wish to have such prayers made henceforth. By this word of God He would teach us that prayer is a matter of the heart. We cannot worship God by "going through the motions" of prayer. The heart must pray first; the lips and members of the body may afterward obey its impulses. It is the heart that

34

prays, never the knees or the hands or the lips. Prayer must be the vent for the fermentation of the heart (H. W. Beecher). "Prayers without the heart's desires are like birds without wings; they never leave the earth, never rise to heaven." (Thomas Guthrie)

And now, having reviewed the essential properties of prayer, we can appreciate all the more that the Lord's Prayer is the model prayer. "There is no nobler prayer on earth than the Lord's Prayer . . . and we should not exchange all the blessings of this earth for it," says Luther. This prayer was modeled by the lips of the Savior Himself in response to the plea of His disciples, "Lord, teach us to pray." Thus it is perfection itself among prayers, and we do well to study a few of its outstanding qualities so that we may learn therefrom how to fashion our own prayers.

The *introductory words* of the Lord's Prayer, "Our Father, who art in heaven," in themselves either embody or imply all the chief elements which go to make up an effectual, God-pleasing prayer. Only he who, by the agency of the Holy Spirit working through the means of grace, has embraced Christ in the true faith can pray the words "Our Father."

There are indeed those who maintain that the Lord's Prayer is one prayer which, contrary to Christ's express wish, was not made in Jesus' name. However, the words "Our Father" imply to us that also this prayer is made in Jesus' name, for all those and only those who can truly address God as Father in this prayer have become His children by virtue of the adoption that has taken place through faith in Jesus as their Redeemer and Mediator; and hence when they recite those words of the Lord's Prayer they are approaching God the Father

35

in Jesus' name, trusting in the reconciliation that has been accomplished by Christ, by which they are enabled to address an otherwise wrathful God with such endearing terms.

The Lord's Prayer contains *seven petitions,* of which the first three and the last three in few words comprehend the entire field of spiritual wants, while the fourth in just seven words asks for the satisfaction of all our temporal needs.

The Second, the Third, and the Fifth Petition deserve special mention, inasmuch as they contain factors of proper prayer. In the Second Petition the praying Christian expresses an unselfishness and other-worldly concern which are foreign to earth-bound and materialistically minded men. The prayer "Thy Kingdom come" refers to God's kingdoms of grace and glory. By these words the faithful Christian requests not only that he himself be included in the Christian church on earth but also that the Lord help him to be instrumental in spreading the Gospel by personal witness, prayer, and support of the church's world mission program. Moreover, in this petition the sincere disciple of Christ gives expression to his yearning to be relieved from the frailties and concerns of this life as he prays the exalted Christ to hasten His return in glory to claim him and all the redeemed for their eternal reunion with Him in the Kingdom of Glory in heaven.

By the Third Petition we are required to pray humbly and in full agreement with God's will, for this petition provides for the enforcement of the Lord's will on earth even as it reigns supreme in heaven. In the Fifth Petition we are reminded of the necessity that all acceptable prayer must flow from a forgiving heart.

The Doxology, which is not found in some manuscripts of the Bible, contains the element of praise and thanks, which so many omit from their prayers but which should be included in all our prayers as a token of gratitude for blessings received. And yet another commendable feature of the Lord's Prayer: its Doxology states the very reason why we should present this prayer with firm confidence in the Gospel's promises concerning prayer: because He to whom this prayer is addressed is at once the Ruler of the kingdom, the Author and Wielder of all power, and the Possessor and Recipient of all glory. Hence He can and will grant our prayer.

How glorious, then, is the Lord's Prayer! It embodies every proper desire of the praying heart. It combines in simple language every divine promise, every human sorrow and want, and every Christian aspiration for the welfare of others. Samuel M. Zwemer remarks in *Taking Hold of God* (pp. 152, 153): "It is the shortest, deepest, richest of all prayers ever offered by man and could only proceed from the lips of Him who knew what was in man because He is the Son of God. . . . It is simple yet always novel; infinitely easy to repeat, yet infinitely hard to understand; humble in its phrases yet exalted in its high significance; natural yet supernatural; the commencement and the climax of all true prayer."

The man who truly prays this prayer is a man of power. When the Christian offers this prayer, "Satan trembles when he sees the weakest Christian on his knees." Never was nor ever shall there be another prayer like it. Let us therefore employ it frequently, fervently, profitably.

IV

INCIDENTAL AIDS TO PRAYER

BASIC requirements for effectual prayer are conformity to the will of the heavenly Father, faith in Christ as Redeemer and Mediator combined with submission to His sovereignty, confidence in the power and validity of prayer, and fervency of heart which only the Holy Spirit can generate. These were treated in the previous chapter. But since the human being is a creature of habit, he may find some additional incidental suggestions helpful in developing the art of prayer.

Manifestly the prayer life of a Christian, as is the case with natural life, is a matter of growth and development. The desire to pray is instinctive in man but requires guidance, training, and practice. The child who has learned simple prayers by rote at its mother's knee must develop into the mature child of God who at the forge of fiery trial refines and fashions an effective instrument and in the academy of adversity learns under the guidance of the Spirit of God how to wield it with dexterity and power. Obviously, prayer is an art which must be learned. As in all fields of skill, there can be little learning without practice.

In the process of becoming proficient in the art of prayer the Christian will find *meditation* helpful. Meditation is the exercise which puts the petitioner in the right frame of mind to pray. Meditation is the ideal preparation for prayer and the base to which it tends to return. To encourage such meditation, Jesus recommends, "When thou prayest, *enter into thy closet,* and when thou hast *shut thy door,* pray to thy Father which is in secret" (Matthew 6:6). The purpose for this is clear. He who would pray will find it advantageous to withdraw from the world and its noisy whirl of activity. The spirit of the busy world around us and the spirit of prayer within us are at odds with each other. For that reason seek privacy as the most conducive atmosphere for prayer.

Meditation, to be most helpful in developing the art of prayer, should be coupled with the reading of Scripture. Within this Book we find the mirror which most clearly and accurately reflects the true nature of both man and God. In it we behold an unsparing revelation of our sins, the hypocrisy of our hearts, the corruption of our souls, the deceitfulness of our flesh, and the weakness of our will. But in it we also find portrayed God's love for mankind, His grace in Christ Jesus, His pardon of sin for the sake of the Crucified One, and His infinite patience with the frailties of His children in Christ. The Scriptures also present to us the sins and failures, the hopes and fears of the saints of God in all ages, and in their lives and experiences we see our own. In Holy Writ are unveiled God's ways with man. Through the Holy Spirit, who speaks to us from the pages of the holy volume, we feel the presence of God within us. Before His eyes nothing is hidden. Our inmost secrets are an open book. This intimate communion with our Lord encourages us to pray, to pray more honestly and fervently, to pray more naturally and confidently.

Combined with proper preparation for prayer must be the consistent *practice* of prayer if the Christian is to master this art. Like any other habit or skill, prayer becomes easier with exercise and repetition. No one is born with this skill perfected. It is achieved gradually, and usually after many misadventures. Though our prayers be only "the burden of a sigh, the falling of a tear," though we have learned only the ABCs of prayer, we can become proficient in its art by careful, conscientious, persistent practice. E. M. Bound wrote in *Purpose in Prayer* (p. 38): "Prayer is a trade to be learned. We must be apprentices and serve our time at it. Painstaking care, much thought, practice and labor are required to be a skillful tradesman in praying. Practice in this, as well as in all other trades, makes perfect. Toiling hands and hearts alone make proficients in this heavenly trade." In the process of achieving proficiency in prayer the Christian will find in Scripture many helpful aids in some inspirational phrase or sentence on which his petition can take wing to the heart of our heavenly Father.

As mentioned elsewhere, another definite asset of prayer is *humility*. The apostles Peter and James both write, "God . . . giveth grace to the humble" (James 4:6; 1 Peter 5:5). The publican's prayer was heard because it was humble, declared Jesus (Luke 18:14). On behalf of the Lord, Isaiah says (66:2): "To this man will I look, even to him that is poor and of a contrite spirit and trembleth at My Word." Such expressions as the "poor" whose "cry" God hears and the "meek" whose "desire" is granted are frequently found in Scripture and assure us that the Lord looks with favor upon the humble prayer. From these and similar passages we may conclude that humility is a valuable aid to prayer.

The Lord warns us not only against the pride of the Pharisee who exalted himself in prayer over his fellow men — particularly the publican, but also against the vain ambition of such as the sons of Zebedee, who desired to rule at either side of Christ in glory. This warning applies also to fantastic requests in prayer, such as petitions for evidence of the power of prayer in signs and wonders, visions and revelations. Such prayers lack faith, just as a lover who desires assurances that he is truly loved by his fiancée doubts the love of his sweetheart. Nothing is more beautiful than the prayer of a Christian whose faith is matched by his humility as a child of God.

Prayer, to be effective, must be *energetic*, fervent. Prayer is not an occasion for dreaming but an act in which the Christian is to summon all the powers of his soul to intense action. It is, in fact, the highest and noblest exercise in which a man can engage. Jacob at Jabbok "wrestled" with the Lord in prayer. Our Savior in the Garden of Gethsemane prayed so earnestly that His perspiration became "as it were great drops of blood falling down to the ground" (Luke 22:44). In the Psalms David frequently uses the words "cry," "cry out," and "cry aloud," to indicate the intensity of his prayers. Elijah also "prayed fervently" to God. Thus by precept and example we are encouraged in Scripture to pray energetically. "The effectual, *fervent* prayer of a righteous man availeth much," says James (5:16). Prayer is an art in which only those become proficient who in faith bend all their energies to the task.

With energy and earnestness in prayer we must also couple *patience*. Energy alone as an aid to prayer might imply that the petitioner relies on himself, his own ability, his goodness, for the efficacy of his petitions. Prayers dare never be an expression of our dependence on our personal influence with God. Prayer, to be the

41

key to the throne room of God, must be offered in a spirit of submission to His will. Patience is the element in Christian prayer which expresses confidence that God will hear and answer our prayers at His time and in His way. The signature of our prayer in the word "Amen" reflects such patient confidence.

Perhaps the most impressive description of prayer in the Old Testament is that of "waiting upon" God. To "wait upon" is not merely passive submission. It is to expect — expect confidently, but also to await patiently. It is to yearn for but not demand impatiently; to expect confidently but not complain at the delay; to agree to yield to the will of the Lord if our wish is not fulfilled but not yield to the temptation to agree that our prayer will not be answered. To pray in that sense is to wait upon the Lord patiently, and this is a distinct aid to the validity of our prayer.

But these suggested aids for prayer are frequently frustrated, at least in part, by the obstacles posed by the weaknesses and perversity of our human nature. Among these hindrances to prayer we find *inattentiveness.*

There are times when even the most faithful disciple of the Lord feels dissatisfied with his prayers. They seem so lifeless and cold. His thoughts insist on wandering when he addresses his petitions to the Almighty. He experiences difficulty in concentrating on his prayers, particularly when no heavy burden presses heavily upon him. This bad intellectual habit of inattention may become a fixed habit if allowed to develop and may seriously impair the validity of our prayers. Therefore Solomon exhorts: "Whatsoever thy hand findeth to do, do it with thy might" (Ecclesiastes 9:10). This wise admonition applies to prayer with as much force as to any other human endeavor.

Another serious hindrance to prayer is *preoccupation* with the pleasures and concerns of life. Modern life is filled to overflowing with activity. The Christian of the twentieth century is tempted to become such an activist that he has little time and less desire for prayer. There is the daily routine of work. The spiraling cost of living compels him to work at two jobs, or his wife must also take up some outside employment, thus disrupting the home. Then there must be time for relaxation, such as bowling, television, cinema, plays, opera, concerts, and the many spectator sports. Add to this parties, clubs, civic and political obligations.

Caught in this constant whirl of activity, the child of God today finds himself so preoccupied with material things and the problems of life that the resultant tensions interfere with his prayer life and deaden his spirituality. It is imperative that we recognize this peril to our soul and free ourselves sufficiently from the demands on our time made by material things to find time for the things of the spirit, among which communion with God in prayer is of major importance. Our Lord Himself admonishes us: "Seek ye first the kingdom of God and His righteousness." (Matthew 6:33)

Also among the deterrents to prayer we find human *pride and self-reliance.* By nature we are slow to learn the lesson of our utter dependence on God. Excellent health, a strong body, intellectual endowments, success, and popularity inflate man's ego. Human pride is a dull scholar in the school of experience. Man's vanity blunts his sense of need of divine help for the problems and emergencies of life. Self-confidence inclines him to look primarily to himself or to other human agencies for the relief of his ills and wants. With this sort of attitude the prayer life suffers.

Even if prayer for such an one has become a fixed habit, the effort becomes strained or listless. The petitioner becomes vexed and disappointed with his prayers. But a few moments of prayerful reflection on the cause for this condition would place the blame where it belongs — upon ourselves, for we cannot do God's work without God's help. With the disciples we must request, "Lord, teach us to pray."

Finally, there is the obstacle of *selfishness*. The spirit of selfishness in prayer leads ultimately to barrenness and frustration. If the petitioner limits his requests to his own individual needs, he restricts the sphere of his prayer life, becomes a spiritual introvert, and gradually destroys the foundation of the valid prayer, which is faith in Christ, the faith that "worketh by love."

Selfish prayer may even include the names of friends and relatives, but if so, it is done in a perfunctory way. Certainly there is no travail of soul for the material and spiritual concerns of others, of which Paul speaks in discussing his prayers. It is Christ's own command that we love others, even our enemies. It follows that our petitions at the Throne of Grace should include also the needs of our fellow men if our prayers are to be offered according to the will of our heavenly Father.

The surest remedy for selfishness in prayer is to engage wholeheartedly in the service of God and of man. As we become involved with the lives of others for Christ's sake, their needs will automatically become a part of our intercessions. Let us pray for the gift of selflessness in prayer and service.

V

Customs in Prayer

IN EVERY age and in every clime there have been those who insist on the detailed observance of form and ceremony in prayer. What are we to make of such customs?

There is, for instance, the use of words in prayer. Are words a necessary concomitant in prayer? This question the Scriptures answer in the negative, both directly and by inference. Psalm 10:17 reads: "Lord, Thou hast heard the *desire* of the humble; Thou wilt prepare their *heart,* Thou wilt cause Thine ear to hear." Nothing is stated here concerning the necessity of words in true prayer.

The essence of prayer is that it is the communion "of the believing heart" with God. Prayer is the flight of the Christian heart to commune with its God. Thus, of Hannah's prayer we read in Scripture: "She spake in her heart; only her lips moved, but her voice was not heard" (1 Samuel 1:13). Moreover, when Moses on the banks of the Red Sea lifted up a prayer for fleeing Israel in their plight as they milled about helpless before Pharaoh's onrushing hordes, we are not told that the prophet uttered so much as one audible word. And yet the Lord said to Moses: "Wherefore criest thou unto Me?" (Exodus 14:15)

Nevertheless, the use of words in prayer is encouraged both by recorded suggestion and by example.

Psalm 19:14 reads: "Let the words of my mouth and the meditation of my heart be acceptable in Thy sight, O Lord, my Strength and my Redeemer." In prayer the heart must, the lips may, pray. For this reason Jesus prescribed the words of the Lord's Prayer as a model for all Christians to follow in the spoken prayer.

The Bible records that the Savior in a number of instances uttered His prayers aloud, particularly when these were offered in public. The father of the lunatic child begged tearfully of Jesus: "Lord, I believe; help Thou mine unbelief" (Mark 9:24). The Syrophenician woman screamed her petition as she followed after Jesus. The entire Psalter is a collection of prayers which may be either spoken or sung to the accompaniment of music.

The use of words in prayer presents a certain advantage. The spoken word assists in riveting our attention on our prayers and by that means serves to intensify the fervency of prayer. And yet the spoken prayer, particularly if memorized, is subject to the same abuse of being performed in perfunctory fashion as are all of man's habitual acts. Witness the lifeless droning or "singsong" manner that characterizes the recitation or reading of prayers in our homes and churches. Probably more often than not this external lethargy is a reflection of inner coldness and indifference in the act of prayer.

Much controversy has raged around the respective merits of extemporaneous, free, or *ex corde* ("out of the heart") prayer on the one hand and the printed or prescribed prayer on the other. Both present certain advantages but also offer peculiar difficulties.

The extemporaneous prayer, when offered by one gifted in the art of prayer, is likely to cause the gathering in whose presence and on whose behalf it is made

46

to follow it more attentively because it is novel and fresh. Novelty holds a certain natural attraction for the human being. Again, the *ex corde* prayer for special or very extraordinary occasions possesses an advantage over the book prayer. The former will likely be more appropriate than the latter, particularly if no prayer may be located in the prayer book or agenda to fit the occasion; for then the extemporaneous prayer will more satisfactorily express the sentiments of the petitioner on that occasion than an ill-fitting prayer from a book. It is obvious, then, that particularly for personal and private use the extemporaneous prayer is advantageous. In this way the petitioner may voice the peculiar problems which weigh upon his heart.

For public purposes, though, if no prayer be found befitting the occasion, it may be preferable to write a special prayer for the event. Never, however, should it be maintained that the public *ex corde* prayer of itself is incontrovertible proof of greater sincerity. In fact, the very opposite is often true, for he who offers the *ex corde* prayer in public is often compelled to search for thoughts and expressions and thus becomes guilty of uttering meaningless platitudes or vain repetitions. This suggests that the chief weakness of the extempore prayer is that it is likely to lack orderly arrangement and fullness. To this may be added the disadvantage that when we are weary or dull, we experience difficulty in composing prayers for ourselves and we desire a convenient prayer of devout words to express the desires of our heart.

In favor of the printed or book prayer we may cite Biblical example. The Psalter was extensively used in Old Testament times as the Jewish prayer book. Moreover, Christ Himself formulated a comprehensive prayer briefly worded for memory's sake. It will fit every occasion and every purpose. Then, too, when the Lord prayed on the cross, He Himself twice made use of memorized prayers which He quoted from the Psalter, the words of Psalm 22:1, "My God, My God, why hast Thou forsaken Me," and of Psalm 31:5, "Into Thy hands I commend My spirit."

Ordinarily the printed or memorized prayer will more fully and accurately express the needs of the heart. And when employed for congregational and public purposes in general, the read prayer has a distinct advantage, for since one of the incidental purposes of public prayer is to instruct and edify the hearer, the book prayer is not likely to contain any improper or misleading expressions. In addition, every Christian has access to a vast fund of simple, stately prayers found in the Catechism, the hymnal, and a great variety of valuable prayer books, which have been and still are the inspiration of thousands of the devout, so that there is little likelihood that an occasion will arise for which no suitable prayer may be found.

And yet there is one danger, already referred to, connected with the use of the written or memorized prayer, and that is sluggishness. To use one prayer or a limited number of prayers with great regularity may lead to listlessness and lifelessness in prayer. It is not only the Romanist, fingering his beads and making his crosses and genuflections, not only the Mohammedan, falling upon his knees and prostrating himself at the call of the muezzin from the minaret, who does not pray but also the Protestant who may say or read his prayers to God and still not be praying.

To summarize, extempore prayers are as much subject to abuse as prayers read from a prayer book or recited from memory. If the latter are exposed to the danger of mechanical recital, the former are liable to vain repetition or straining after effect. In making his choice of the two, the praying Christian should bear in mind his own aptitude, the place, and the occasion. Probably it would be advisable to use neither form of prayer to the complete exclusion of the other. Both possess distinct advantages and should freely be used by the Christian as the occasion appears to require.

The number and choice of words in prayer do not contribute anything to the validity of prayer in the sight of God. It has well been said: God does not look at the arithmetic of our prayers, how many words there be; nor does He look at the rhetoric, how beautiful the expressions in prayer may be; nor does He look at the logic of our prayers, how methodical and nicely arranged they may be. What He looks at is the sincerity of our prayers, how earnest they are.

Luther has nicely summarized the attitude of Scripture toward the number of words to be employed in prayer in his remark: "The fewer the words, the better the prayer." The Savior once warned his disciples concerning prayer: "When ye pray, use not vain repetitions, as the heathen do; for they think that they shall be heard for their much speaking" (Matthew 6:7). And then He adds (v. 8): "For your Father knoweth what things ye have need of before ye ask Him." It would be to regard the Lord of Glory as in a general class with the heathen gods to overwhelm Him with a multitude of words when we pray. Thereupon Jesus proceeds to provide the disciples with a model for prayer, the Lord's Prayer, a prayer which is a pattern for brevity but also for comprehensiveness, a prayer which is so rich in content that it embraces all our spiritual and temporal needs.

If additional examples of brief prayers in Scripture are desired, witness the brevity of the majority of the psalms; the prayer of King Hezekiah (Isaiah 38); the petition for the nobleman's son (John 4:47-49); the prayer of the Savior in the Garden (Matthew 26); the prayer of the apostles which resulted in the selection of Matthias to complete the circle of the Twelve (Acts 1:24, 25); the prayer of the congregation at Jerusalem in behalf of Peter (Acts 4:24-30), etc.

For ordinary purposes, then, the rule may be established in the words of Luther: "The more numerous the words, the worse the prayer. Few words and much meaning is Christian; many words and little meaning is heathen." As John Bunyan once remarked, "In prayer it is better to have a heart without words than words without a heart."

And yet the conclusion should not be reached that longer prayers are altogether incorrect nor that those who are spiritually sluggish are justified in making their prayers as short as possible. The Scriptures also record longer prayers, e. g., many of the psalms and the High-priestly Prayer of Jesus (John 17). Our prayers should be comprehensive, but in this connection we are concerned chiefly with correcting the impression that prayers must be wordy in order to please God on high.

The rhetoric of prayer is merely incidental. If the heart be properly attuned to the will of God, words will be found with which adequately to express the desires of the heart. Even though the words in such a prayer be not of the choicest nor the grammatical structure above reproach, *if the heart be sincere and attuned to the true God, God will understand and accept the prayer.* Ours is the promise made in Romans 8:27: "He that searcheth the hearts knoweth what is the mind of the Spirit, because He maketh intercession for the saints according to the will of God."

However, the Christian at all times should be mindful that in prayer he is communing with God and consequently ought not be careless with his prayers. Biblical words and expressions are especially to be commended, for they are the words which the Lord Himself has provided. The use of beautiful and expressive language in public prayers may be commended if thereby he who leads in prayer would encourage and stimulate the devotion of those in the prayer circle. Otherwise, however, it has no particular value.

From time immemorial much stress has been laid on the importance of posture in prayer, particularly in non-Christian religions. In their minute regulations of public and private prayer all the great non-Christian religions of today place great emphasis on the right posture. The most pronounced illustration of this is to be found among the Mohammedans, where the faithful in the mosque worship are arranged in ranks and prostrate themselves with such a variety of genuflections, movements of the arms, and manipulations of the fingers that all this impresses the onlooker as being a prayer drill rather than spiritual worship.

But also among Christians various habits are observed at prayer. Some stand; others sit; still others lie on their backs, kneel, or prostrate themselves in prayer. Again, there are those who look heavenward in prayer, while others bow their heads or close their eyes. Many are accustomed to folding their hands; others clasp them behind their backs; still others lift them up outstretched to heaven; while additional others shield their eyes in prayer.

What general rule should be followed relative to such posture in prayer? Which of these customs is to be preferred?

Let us note well: God's Word makes no prescription in such matters. It is true that the apostle Paul writes (1 Timothy 2:8): "I will therefore that men pray everywhere, lifting up holy hands without wrath and doubting." The emphasis here, however, lies on the "holy hands" which were customarily lifted up in token of prayer. And yet there often is a certain value in posture. There can be no doubt that, particularly in the case of small children, the practice of closing the eyes, folding the hands, and bowing the head helps to shut out distractions and fix the attention of the individual on the subject of prayer. As a suggestion in this regard, many Sunday schools observe the custom of introducing prayers with the following rhyme:

> Our hands we fold,
> Our heads we bow,
> Ready to talk
> To Jesus now.

Obviously, slovenly habits of posture are not conducive to fervent prayer. If, therefore, a certain posture contributes to devotion at prayer, it is highly commendable. Nevertheless, it should be noted that the most pious attitude in prayer will never guarantee that the thoughts will not wander.

The particular form or ceremony of prayer is in itself a matter of choice. Scriptural examples may be found for nearly all the personal habits in prayer enumerated previously. Moses lifted up his hands when praying. Abraham and the publican assumed a standing attitude while praying. Stephen knelt in prayer, a position to which both David and St. Paul allude. The leper and Christ in Gethsemane prostrated themselves. Luther in his writing inclines toward the folding of hands when he remarks: "The children and servants should approach the table with folded hands and in orderly manner." Let each choose the particular posture which appeals to him most, but let him also bear in mind that not the habit in itself but devotion and fervency of heart is at all times the real motive prompting the assumption of any posture in prayer.

The advice which Luther offers (St. Louis VIII, 748) is in full accord with the Word of God: "It does not matter whether we stand, kneel, or lie prostrate; for all these, being external matters, are immaterial since they are neither commanded nor forbidden, as also others, for instance, lifting up the head and eyes to heaven, folding the hands, and smiting upon one's breast. Yet they should not be despised, since Scripture, yes, Christ Himself, praises them, Ephesians 3:14; 1 Timothy 2:8; John 17:1. So also it is not wrong if, for instance, one who is binding sheaves in a field or who is lying in bed should pray only with the heart."

VI

The Scope of Prayer

IN ORDER to pray we must know for what to pray. We spiritually ignorant and blinded human beings often know not for what we should pray. For instance, the wife of Zebedee besought the Lord to give her two sons a place in His kingdom, one to His left, the other to His right. This petition He was compelled to reject because she was not aware of the nature of the thing for which she prayed. So also we must plead, "Lord, teach us to pray." (Luke 11:1)

The scope of prayer is indeed vast and comprehensive. It includes "everything that tends to the glory of God and to our own and our neighbor's welfare, both spiritual and bodily blessings."

Paul writes (Philemon 4:6): "Be careful for nothing; but in everything by prayer and supplication with thanksgiving let your requests be made known unto God." All cares and worries either for temporal or for spiritual exigencies are sinful. Whatever the need or the plight, the best advice available is that which the apostle offers in 1 Peter 5:7: "Cast all your care upon Him, for He careth for you." Even as Christians we are constantly in need of the Scriptural reminder, "Every good gift and every perfect gift is from above and cometh down from the Father of lights" (James 1:17). Therefore everything that is in agreement with the will of the Lord may form the burden of our prayer. (1 John 5:14)

All things may be classified as either temporal or spiritual gifts. As temporal and spiritual gifts are not of the same order, so a distinction must be observed in making our requests for them. For such spiritual blessings as are necessary for our salvation we are to ask without any condition or limitation, since they are in full agreement with the good and gracious will of God, whose "good pleasure" it is "to give you the Kingdom." On the other hand, when we pray for temporal gifts, we must attach the condition: "If it be Thy will or serve Thy glory and my welfare." Temporal gifts are not at all necessary for our salvation, which after all should be our chief interest in life, as the Savior admonishes us (Matthew 6:33), "Seek ye first the kingdom of God and His righteousness; and all these things shall be added unto you." On the contrary, there are many apparently highly desirable things in life which for us would act as a snare and pitfall. Therefore we, who as foolish children do not fully realize the nature of our requests or their possible effect on us, should in our petitions for material things commit the answer to our prayer to the hands of the omniscient God, who knows and sees everything, even the potential consequences for us of the gifts we desire, and say: "Not my will but Thine be done."

For such action in prayer we have an abundance of Biblical illustrations. Thus did the leper plead for the cure of his disease, Matthew 8:2, "Lord, *if Thou wilt,* Thou canst make me clean." Jesus Himself in Gethsemane is a blessed example for the conditioned prayer when He cries (Luke 22:42), "Father, *if Thou be willing,* remove this cup from Me; *nevertheless not My will but Thine be done.*"

If we pray after this manner, our prayer shall be heard. However, this does not imply that God gratifies our every wish. Our wishes may not always be for our own good, and no one knows this better than the all-knowing God, who loves us too well to supply us with foolish or hurtful gifts. Thus we may pray for prosperity, but it never arrives. We pray for the recovery of a sick child or friend, for the removal of a cross or burden, but our heart's desire is not granted. We do not obtain that particular gift, but if we keep on praying, God invariably gives us something better, something which according to His purpose is for our highest possible benefit; and that constitutes His answer to our prayer. When Paul implored the Lord for the removal of the "thorn" in his flesh, God answered his petition thus: "My grace is sufficient for thee, for My strength is made perfect in weakness" (2 Corinthians 12:9). Our prayer never comes home weeping. We get what we ask, or rather what we should have asked. Therefore we say with the poet Melissander:

> Lord, as Thou wilt, deal Thou with me;
> No other wish I cherish.
> In life and death I cling to Thee;
> O Lord, let me not perish!
> Let but Thy grace ne'er from me part,
> Else as Thou wilt; grant patient heart:
> Thy will the best is ever.

Material gifts, for which we ask conditionally, are: "Those which are necessary for the welfare of the body and the sustenance of life, such as: good health, riches, skill, wisdom, beauty, food, clothing, and countless other things." (Dietrich, Catechism, qu. 347)

In contradistinction from such temporal gifts are the spiritual blessings which are defined in the same book: "Those which are necessary for the welfare of the soul and for the attainment of life eternal, such as: forgiveness of sins, God's grace, justification, renewal, governance of the Holy Spirit, constancy in faith, and steadfastness in tribulation." (Dietrich, Catechism, qu. 346)

Such spiritual gifts are necessary for our salvation, and hence we ask for them without the addition of any condition to our prayer. But we mortals, breathing as we do the atmosphere of this present world, are likely to overlook the value of these spiritual gifts and hence need constant prodding and spurring to make us realize that we should ask for them. What a glorious privilege is ours to request spiritual gifts in their great variety and infinite vastness without any limitation whatsoever! No spiritual need is so great that we dare not confidently take it to the Lord in prayer; no want is so small and insignificant that He will refuse to incline His ear and listen attentively.

> Have we trials and temptations?
> Is there trouble anywhere?
> We should never be discouraged,
> Take it to the Lord in prayer.
> Can we find a Friend so faithful,
> Who will all our sorrows share?
> Jesus knows our every weakness —
> Take it to the Lord in prayer.
>
> — Joseph Scriven

If we pray in this spirit, we shall experience that prayer is the dove which, when sent out, returns bringing with it the olive leaf; namely, peace of heart. Prayer is David's harp before which the evil spirit flees. (Johann Gerhard)

Ordinarily the praying Christian need not be urged to pray for himself. The consciousness of his own material and spiritual needs as well as the selfishness which still is inherent in the nature of even the most advanced Christian will incite him to address prayers in his own behalf to the Author and Giver of every good and perfect gift. But Christians often *do* require exhortation to pray for others. "A man's prayer for others is a very fair thermometer of his own religious condition" (Maclaren). Such *intercessory prayer is commanded in Scripture.* St. James writes (5:16), "Pray one for another." No one should say with Cain, "Am I my brother's keeper?" And these intercessions, if made by Christians with a fervent spirit, have the promise of great power, for in the same verse we find the statement: "The effectual fervent prayer of a righteous man availeth much." Let us therefore be encouraged not only to pray for ourselves but also to intercede for others in their material and spiritual emergencies.

In our prayers for others it is but natural that we should first of all think of our immediate families, of our relatives, of our friends and acquaintances. And it is quite proper to intercede concernedly for all of those who are near and dear to us, particularly if one of them be in a sad spiritual state, as, for instance, a godless parent, a profligate child, a worthless relative, or a spiritually bankrupt friend. For prayer in which the petitioner seeks to usurp all the resources of God for the satisfaction of his own greed and vanity, there is no promised reward. However, for prayer that asks God to grant its requests for *His glory* and the *neighbor's welfare* there is the glorious promise of prevailing power.

The day was long, the burden I had borne
Seemed more than I could bear,
And then it lifted — but I did not know
Someone had knelt in prayer,

Had taken me to God that very hour
And asked the easing of the load, and He,
In infinite compassion, had stooped down
And taken it from me.

We cannot tell how often as we pray
For some bewildered one, hurt and distressed,
The answer comes — but many times those hearts
Find sudden peace and rest.

Someone had prayed, and Faith, a reaching hand,
Took hold of God and brought Him down that day!
So many, many hearts have need of prayer —
Oh, let us pray.
　　　　　　　　　　　　　　— Grace Noll Crowell

In our prayers we should include also our *church,*
both the members of the congregation and our fellow
Christians everywhere. When the apostle James wrote
the words "Pray one for another," he was referring
primarily to fellow Christians. In Galatians 6:10 Paul
admonishes: "Let us do good unto all men, *especially
unto them who are of the household of faith."* One
means of doing "good unto them," probably the greatest
of all, is to pray for them. Therefore, each time we
pray the General Prayer we think of our Christian
brethren when we say: "Most heartily we beseech Thee
so to rule and govern Thy Church Universal, with all
its pastors and ministers, that it may be preserved in
the pure doctrine of Thy saving Word."

Thus Christian prayer should reach out beyond the
confines of the local congregation and embrace the needs

of the church at large, its educational institutions, and its Gospel ministry far and near. The Lord Jesus exhorts in Matthew 9:37, 38, "The harvest truly is plenteous, but the laborers are few; pray ye therefore the Lord of the harvest that He will send forth laborers into His harvest." Also, St. Paul writes (Ephesians 6:18): "Praying always with all prayer and supplication in the Spirit and watching thereunto with all perseverance and supplication for all saints." The welfare of the saints, that is, of our fellow Christians, should ever be a matter of our great concern.

Again, as Christians pray for one another, so also they do not neglect to make intercession for mankind in general, especially for the government. To this end we find the explicit charge of St. Paul recorded, 1 Timothy 2:1, 2, "I exhort therefore that, first of all, supplications, prayers, intercessions, and giving of thanks be made for all men; for kings and for all that are in authority." In these critical times when our government is compelled to attack economic, social, and political problems of the most serious character, its troubles and concerns invite our most sincere and earnest prayers. In this guided-missile age our country is in a state of unrest and insecurity. There are multitudes of strikes in widely scattered areas. Subversive activities on the part of Communism and the underworld, and corruption in government, business, and labor continue throughout the land. Thus we might continue to enumerate an almost endless list of governmental problems. Who, then, would deny that the government as well as all mankind is in need of the fervent prayer of righteous men which availeth much?

Even our enemies should properly be the beneficiaries of our prayers. Christ commands us to pray for our enemies (Matthew 5:44): "Love your enemies, bless them that curse you, do good to them that hate you, and *pray for them which despitefully use you and per-secute you."* A surpassingly beautiful illustration of prayer for enemies is afforded by our Savior on the cross when He pleads (Luke 23:34), "Father, forgive them; for they know not what they do." To pray for and to forgive one's enemies is the acid test of Christianity in practice; but with God's grace and strength Christians find it possible, as is proved by the example of Stephen, who in the hour of death prayed for those who stoned him, as is recorded in Acts 7:60: "And he kneeled down and cried with a loud voice, Lord, lay not this sin to their charge."

Only one exception is to be made to the sweeping generalization that Christians ought to pray for all men, and that one exception is the dead. When the apostle Paul exhorts (1 Timothy 2:1-4) that intercessions should be made for all men, he admittedly is referring only to living persons. Search as we will, we shall not find one divine command to pray for the departed, not one divine promise that such a prayer is heard, not one example of such an act in all the canonical books of the Bible. The passage to which some point in support of prayers for the dead is located in the apocryphal writing, 2 Maccabees 12:43-45, which contains no command to make intercession for the dead but merely records that a certain Judas with pious intent prayed for the deceased. Opposed to this single passage from a questionable source are the hosts of passages from the canonical writings which imply that it is unnecessary, vain, and foolish to pray for the dead. Therefore this practice should assiduously be avoided.

VII

THE PLACE FOR PRAYER

THE PLACE for prayer is an optional matter. The Christian may hold audience with God wherever he chooses. All places are acceptable to God; in fact, all places should remind the believer of the duty and glorious privilege of prayer. Therefore St. Paul enjoins all believers (1 Timothy 2:8): "I will therefore that men pray *everywhere*." The holy men of the Bible found occasion to pray in many places. Peter prayed on a housetop, Paul in prison, Jonah in the fish's belly, Daniel in the lions' den.

The Lord is everywhere, and His ear is ever alert to the sigh of the heart or to the cry of anguish from the lips of a believer engaged in prayer wherever he may be. Go where we will, to the snow-capped crest of a mountain peak or to the nethermost depths of the sea, to the impenetrable fastnesses of the wilderness or to the busiest street intersection of the most densely populated metropolis, to the oppressively silent wastes of the desert or to the turbulent, roaring waters of the giant cataract, God is there to hear our prayer. As you rush to the scene of your labor in the morning or rest in the heat of the afternoon sun beneath the cool shade of the fence-row tree or ponder over plans at an executive's desk, your heart can go out in devotion to God.

And yet, although all places are acceptable to God, not all places are alike for prayer. As in other areas of human activity, so also in our prayer life we form habits. Some places are more attractive to us for prayer purposes than others because of their atmosphere, their association, or their solitude. In these places we are more conscious than elsewhere of the presence and power of God, and here we feel the urge to commune with Him in prayer.

Foremost of such prayer-stimulating places is the church. David gives us a pious example of the church prayer when he exults: "In the congregations will I bless the Lord" (Psalm 26:12). The sermon, while it is the most essential ingredient, is not the only part of public worship. The prayers and the hymns, which are for the most part prayers to the accompaniment of music, are the worshiper's part of every service. Nor should prayer in the church be confined to the altar. It should be spoken likewise in the pew.

Here in God's temple the Christian soul should find a spot where amidst the material distractions of this life it may regularly commune with its God and where, winging itself "above the sordidness and perversity of this earth, it can bathe in the invigorating atmosphere of a nobler world and draw inspiration for the affairs of life" in sweet conversation with its Maker. How appropriate, therefore, it would be if — particularly in our city congregations — the church edifices would remain open all hours of the day for the accommodation of those members or guests who wish to tear themselves away from the distracting influences of the rush and din of everyday life for a few moments of undisturbed communion with God.

But the church is not the only place where, because of its nature as the house of God, the Christian finds a special appeal to pray. The privacy of the *home* also stimulates to prayer. Here in the quiet of his room, apart from all the disturbing factors of modern life, the Christian may concentrate his thoughts and call upon the Lord in prayer. The Savior encourages private prayer when He directs (Matthew 6:6): "Thou, when thou prayest, enter into thy closet, and when thou hast shut thy door, pray to thy Father which is in secret." Thus Daniel was wont to hurry home from the excitement of the court to kneel down and worship his God in undisturbed prayer. May all Christians today follow his devout example!

When a dwelling place is being occupied for the first time or when a young couple is establishing their home, the following or some similar prayer may be spoken:

PRAYER FOR THE HOME

Walk through the rooms of this house, dear Lord,
Making them fair and sweet;
May every wall know the touch of Thy hand,
Each floor the print of Thy feet.

Help us to look through Thine eyes, dear Lord,
To stand at our windows and see
Not commonplace people who walk the streets
But souls who have need of Thee.

Kindle a fire on our hearth, dear Lord,
Warming all who may come.
Build Thou an altar where prayers shall rise,
For prayer is the heart of the home.

Sit at our table with us, dear Lord,
Making each meal a feast,
Breaking the bread and pouring the wine,
Our Host and our Guest and our Priest.

Dwell in the rooms of our house, dear Lord,
Making them sweet and fair,
Till even the passer-by will say,
"The blessed Lord Jesus lives there!"

— Martha Snell Nicholson

Surely a Christian home should be a home of prayer.

Private prayer, to be fervent and earnest, seeks solitude. And so, besides the church and the home, there is the seclusion which out-of-the-way spots in nature afford that invites prayer. The Lord Jesus was accustomed to seek solitude for prayer. On occasion He would go up into a mountain, enter into the Garden of Gethsemane, or wander out into the wilderness to pray. So also the saints of all ages have talked with God in solitary places. Isaac worshiped God in the open field; Elijah prayed on the top of Mt. Carmel and spoke with Jehovah at the mouth of the cave; John communed with Him in the spirit on the Lord's day in the seclusion of the Isle of Patmos.

Today, too, the Christian may in some quiet or awe-inspiring spot of nature find that solitude which is so conducive to heart-to-heart communion with God. As an unknown author has said: "Let us strive completely to shut out the buzz of worldly thoughts when we pray. In prayer our heart should not look like the surface of a lake alive with restless waves and whitecaps but like a body of water, which, with never a ripple to

65

disturb the image, mirrors heaven in its calmness." (*Concordia Pulpit*, VII, 309)

Lest a misunderstanding arise over what has been said, it should still be noted that God has prescribed no certain place for prayer. In Old Testament times the Jews were compelled by the Ceremonial Law to worship at stated times in the temple at Jerusalem. But with the advent of Christ the Ceremonial Law with all of its requirements and limitations has been set aside.

Christ predicted the abolition of the provisions relating to the worship at the temple in Jerusalem when, in His conversation with the Samaritan woman at Jacob's Well concerning the controversy that raged between the Jews and the Samaritans as to the accepted place of worship, He declared: "Woman, believe Me, the hour cometh, when ye shall neither in this mountain nor yet at Jerusalem worship the Father. . . . But the hour cometh and now is, when the true worshipers shall worship the Father in spirit and in truth" (John 4:21-23). Jesus points out that it is not of prime importance where we pray but how we pray and to whom we pray. The place at which prayer happens to be made contributes no value to the efficacy of prayer, as Luther has well said: "No one dare say that prayer in the church is better or is more readily heard than [prayer] in the field or at some other place" (St. Louis XI, 2070). All depends on the spirit of prayer.

VIII

The Time for Prayer

JUST AS the Lord does not regard one place as more acceptable than another for prayer purposes, so also He has given us no command as to specific times when we must pray.

The exhortations in Holy Scripture concerning the time of prayer are general in character. In fact, we are admonished to pray at all times. 1 Thessalonians 5:17 reads: "Pray without ceasing." Again, Luke 18:1 relates that Jesus spoke a parable to encourage men *"always to pray and not to faint."* Paul admonishes (Ephesians 6:18): "Praying always with all prayer and supplication in the Spirit."

It has been said, "Prayer is the Christian's vital breath." We must breathe to live. Once we cease to breathe we die. Just so, for a Christian to discontinue breathing spiritually in prayer would indicate that he is spiritually dead. Not to pray stamps him as a non-Christian. A Christian lives a life of prayer, for he is always in such a state of spirit that he is constantly communing with his God. Since true prayer is the fruit of the believer's faith, the Christian is in ceaseless communion with God and prays even when he is not aware of it. Thus he prays "always," "without ceasing."

What it means "to pray without ceasing" was once beautifully illustrated by a maid named Mary. She said:

"When I open my eyes in the morning, I pray, 'Lord, open the eyes of my understanding'; and while I am dressing, I pray that I may be clothed with the robe of righteousness; and as I begin to work, I pray that I may have strength equal to my day. When I begin to kindle the fires, I pray that God's work may revive in my soul; as I sweep the house, I pray that my heart may be cleaned from all its impurities; while preparing and partaking of breakfast, I desire to be fed with the hidden manna and the sincere milk of the Word; when I am busy with the little children, I look up to God as my Father and pray for the Spirit of adoption that I may be His child; and so on all the day. Everything I do furnishes me with a thought for prayer." (W. Ziethe in *Concordia Pulpit*, VII, 311, 312)

General Stonewall Jackson once said: "I have so fixed the habit [of prayer] in my own mind that I never raise a glass of water to my lips without asking God's blessing. I never seal a letter without putting a word of prayer under the seal. I never take a letter from the post without a brief sending of my thoughts heavenward. I never change my classes in the section-room without a minute's petition for the cadets who go out and those who come in" (*Concordia Pulpit*, VII, 311). John Quincy Adams, despite a very active life, found time to pray an hour daily, usually between four and five in the morning.

Luther, who was far busier than the average modern man who complains so much of lack of time for prayer, puts such as offer this specious excuse to shame when he writes: "I am so busy now that, if I did not spend two or three hours each day in prayer, I could not get through the day."

From these examples the unprejudiced mind is forced to conclude that to "pray without ceasing" is not at all impossible, rather is absolutely necessary in our modern, streamlined, space-minded age. Luther writes: "We Christians are in duty bound to pray without ceasing, if not with the mouth (as we cannot always do), at least with the heart." (Erlangen edition, III, 441)

Once Sir Walter Raleigh came, as he had frequently done before, to Queen Elizabeth of England with a certain petition. The queen, somewhat irked, remarked, "Sir Raleigh, when will you ever stop to approach me with petitions?" Raleigh without hesitation replied, "When the queen will stop to grant me my petitions." So it should be with all Christians. As long as the promise of our heavenly Father and sovereign God, "It shall be given you," continues to stand, we should pray without ceasing. (*Concordia Pulpit*, VII, 312)

While the true Christian is actually praying "without ceasing," even at times when he is not conscious of it, there are certain times which prompt to prayer more than others. Such times are especially times of adversity, times of calamity, such as are described in the General Prayer of the church: "false and pernicious doctrine," "war and bloodshed," "plague and pestilence," "calamity by fire and water," "hail and tempest," "failure of harvest and famine," "anguish of heart," especially over the loss through death or apostasy of one of our loved ones, "despair of God's mercy," etc. Then particularly is the Christian driven to his knees and compelled to beg for mercy and strength.

Even the rank infidel will then at times seek solace in an unavailing attempt at prayer. It is related of Volney, one of those frothy and foulmouthed atheists who trumpet into the world that there is no God and that faith in Him is a vain delusion, that one day he went sailing on the unruffled surface of Lake Erie. But the scene changed. The heavens began to scowl; the deep became greatly agitated. A dreadful storm broke loose threatening all aboard the frail schooner with destruction. And lo, there on the deck of the dismantled vessel, with hands uplifted and tears streaming, knelt the erstwhile notorious infidel, imploring God for mercy. The tempest had dissipated his finespun speculations like so many cobwebs and had brought him to his knees in humble "prayer." (Buchheimer, *From Advent to Advent*, p. 173). Like Volney, many have been forced to "pray" in times of stress. Others flee instinctively to God in times of need.

When the Christian King Gustavus Adolphus of Sweden landed on the shores of Germany with his troops during the Thirty Years' War, it is said that he led his troops in prayer on bended knee, remarking, "The more one prays, the more one conquers. For to have prayed well is half the victory. The best Christian is always the best soldier." And what Gustavus Adolphus did in a time of emergency is characteristic of Christians in general. Thus writes the prophet Isaiah (26:16): "Lord, in trouble have they visited Thee; they poured out a prayer when Thy chastening was upon them." Times of adversity contribute to our spiritual benefit if from them we learn to pray oftener, more fervently, and more humbly.

But also in days of health and good fortune we should not neglect to call upon the name of the Lord. Scripture does not command any specific time or hour of prayer. Nevertheless, since man is largely a "crea-

70

ture of habit," it is advantageous to set aside certain times in the daily routine for prayer. We have examples of such prayer habits among men of God in Bible times. David prayed at evening, morning, and noon. Of Daniel we hear (6:10): "He kneeled upon his knees three times a day and prayed." There is a certain natural propriety in thus addressing God thrice daily. Three times a day we are accustomed to feed our bodies, and this usage certainly should remind us of a similar necessity of giving attention to the welfare of our immortal souls.

Again, the Bible tells us that it was the custom of the saints to pray whenever undertaking some important task. The early Christians were exemplary in their discharge of regularity in prayer. Surely it is the will of God that we should follow the pattern they have set for us. We should pray at least in the morning, in the evening, and before and after meals.

Where is the Christian who in the morning can rise from his bed without thanking the Lord for deliverance from all evil during the night and also for his waking? As he goes forth from his home, not knowing what the day may have in store for him, conscious of his frailty and weakness, realizing the dangers and temptations to which he is constantly exposed, how can a Christian commence the day without first lifting his heart to God and committing himself to the gracious care of his Creator, whose strength and protection he so much requires? Also during the course of the day there are many transactions which invite his prayerful consultation with the all-wise Ruler of the universe — many false steps, many transgressions which require forbearance on the part of the Savior and His forgiveness. Who is

71

there, then, who cannot find a few moments during the day to approach the Throne of Grace? And finally, how can a Christian with a clear conscience retire without thanking God for preservation during the day and without imploring His divine protection during the many hours of the night? Who is there who can resign himself to sleep, the emblem of death, without saying a few words of Christian committal?

Nor should the Christian neglect to invoke divine grace when seating himself at the table or to return thanks before getting up after his meal. And yet there are countless homes in Christian circles where members of the family partake of a meal without so much as pausing to ask God's blessing. No one should seek to excuse this omission with the retort that prayer at meals is not specifically commanded in Holy Scripture. While there is no explicit injunction by our Lord or His apostles to pray at mealtime, there are numerous instances when Jesus prayed at meals, e. g., when He blessed the loaves and the fishes before distributing them to the five thousand, gave thanks over the bread and the wine at the institution of the Lord's Supper, and blessed the bread as He broke it with the Emmaus disciples. There are blessings, direct and indirect, which rest upon the pious and time-honored custom of mealtime prayers, which no household can afford to forgo. Never, therefore, permit this cherished custom to lapse into disuse.

Although no fixed hours for prayer are prescribed in Holy Writ, the blessings derived from regularity should prompt Christians voluntarily to adopt definite habits in prayer.

IX

The Command to Pray

THE BELIEVER who prays consistently according to Scriptural precept and example is veritably compelled by the wealth of material and spiritual blessings he experiences as a result of prayer to cultivate the more abundant prayer life.

However, the average Christian is patently not an ideal or a model of prayer relationship with his heavenly Father and hence frequently fails to seek or to receive the maximum blessings which prayer may and will bestow upon the suppliant. Therefore it becomes necessary to produce additional proof of the power of prayer in order to convince him that prayer should play a more prominent role in his life. Accordingly, we must consider the ever-recurring question "Why should I pray?" — the question which our doubting reason and sluggish flesh puts to us not only in days of health and happiness but also in the dark hours of affliction. So we shall next examine the reasons for prayer.

The first factor which should prompt the believer to commune with his God diligently is the Scriptural command to pray. God has directed all men to pray, as Scripture clearly teaches — Psalm 50:15: "Call upon Me in the day of trouble"; Matthew 4:10: "Thou shalt worship the Lord thy God"; Matthew 7:7: "Ask, and it shall be given you; seek, and ye shall find; knock, and it shall be opened unto you"; Matthew 26:41: "Watch and pray, that ye enter not into temptation"; Ephesians 6:18: "Pray always with all prayer and supplication in the Spirit"; 1 Thessalonians 5:17: "Pray without ceasing"; 1 Timothy 2:1: "I exhort therefore that, first of all, supplications, prayers, intercessions, and giving of thanks be made for all men." Many other passages might be cited, but these will suffice to prove that it is the express will of God that the Christian should pray. In addition there are the examples which Christ and the men of God both in the Old and in the New Testament have given to impress upon us the inescapable duty to pray.

In view of this clearly revealed divine command, where is the Christian who dares question that he *must* pray? Knowing how the Scriptures by direct charge and example exhort men to pray, who dares to endeavor to discover excuses for sluggishness in prayer?

Let it be pointed out clearly and unmistakably that whoever does not pray, *sins* — sins against God's exalted will just as unquestionably as he that robs and kills. Furthermore, whoever is sluggish and indifferent in praying is the victim of his own sinful nature. Many refuse to believe that laxity of prayer is an undeniable transgression of the Second Commandment and as such is sin. Under no circumstances dare we approve the opinion, frequently expressed, that prayer is an optional matter which one may perform or neglect at will. God's Word clearly presents the divine command to pray, so that for everyone prayer becomes a duty which he cannot evade without committing a grievous sin.

However, the Christian's ever-present sinful flesh is constantly on the alert to discover new and original excuses with which to escape this God-given duty to pray. One of the excuses for not being more active in prayer, characteristic of our modern age, is the contention commonly expressed: "I do not have time." This excuse has already been answered under the topic "The Time for Prayer." In addition to what was there stated the observation may be made that despite the many activities of the modern man and woman there are still 1,440 minutes each day to be spent at one's discretion. Who dares, therefore, truthfully to claim that among those he cannot find a few for private and family prayer?

Again, human reason is quick to rush to the assistance of the man who tries to find an excuse for not praying at all or not praying as he should, by raising the objection: "Do you think God actually answers prayer? Are you really persuaded that God at times suspends the operation of the laws of nature to grant a prayer? Can you truly feel that the Almighty God is influenced by your insignificant prayer? Is not prayer an impertinence in the sight of God, who knows what you have need of even before you ask Him?"

These and other similar questions have a common nucleus of thought in that they center in the skeptic's denial of the efficacy of prayer. For example, a writer in the March 13, 1935, issue of the *Christian Century* speaks of prayer as follows: "Baldly stated: the views about God and the nature of the universe have changed. The element of petition in prayer . . . is a relic of the day when people actually did believe that God intervened directly to aid His friends and discomfit His enemies. . . . Our changed ideas of God make it impossible for us to believe in the efficacy of our prayers as we once did."

The modern skeptic expects to be able to analyze prayer and all spiritual truths in the same fashion as a chemist goes about the measurement and isolation of all the elements of the substance he holds in his test tube in the laboratory. But all such pseudoscientific objections fall to the ground if we only have faith in the testimony of God's infallible Word and in the experiences of power which men of prayer have made since the world began. W. Douglas Mackenzie, author of *Paternoster Sheen; or, Light on Man's Destiny*, writes anent these objections (p. 57): "No conceivable calculation of probable coincidences will account for the enormous, the incalculable mass of evidence that human beings can live, and do live, in such relations with God that He acts upon them . . . in terms of their prayer life. The evidence is immeasurable; I say, it is universal."

Whatever other objections our Old Adam and human reason may originate, the truth remains: God has commanded prayer, and whoever refuses to abide by the Lord's will thereby exposes himself to the wrath and curse of God.

And yet we should not view the fact that we *must* pray through the eyes of the old Adam, who regards this matter as a dreary and burdensome duty, but rather through the eyes of the new man, who looks upon prayer as a blessed privilege. If we view prayer in this manner, our sentiment must certainly be: "Thank God that I *may* pray."

Witness the gracious contrast that exists in prayer: God is holiness personified, we are miserable sinners; He is the Supreme Majesty, we but worthless creatures, dust and ashes. Had God not ordained prayer, had He not Himself granted this privilege, how could we ever dare to lift up our hands to heaven in prayer? But thank God, He not only *permits* us to come before His throne with our petitions, He also graciously *commands* us to bring our troubles to Him in prayer.

X

The Promised Answer

AGAIN, if alongside God's command to us to pray we consider His gracious promise to answer prayer, we are prompted all the more to regard prayer as a precious privilege. Consider the fact that the same God who has commanded in Psalm 50:15, "Call upon Me in the day of trouble," has also added the promise: "I will deliver thee, and thou shalt glorify Me." Again, Psalm 145:18, 19, David declares: "The Lord is nigh unto all them that call upon Him, to all that call upon Him in truth. He will fulfill the desire of them that fear Him; He also will hear their cry and will save them." The prophet Isaiah writes (65:24): "And it shall come to pass that, before they call, I will answer; and while they are yet speaking, I will hear." Matthew 7:7, 8 we read the promise of the Savior: "Ask, and it shall be given you; seek, and ye shall find; knock, and it shall be opened unto you." In John 16:23 God guarantees with an oath: "Verily, verily, I say unto you, Whatsoever ye shall ask the Father in My name, He will give it you." Once again, do not conclude that these passages exhaust the Scripture promises of rewarded prayer, but they should suffice.

God promises to hear and answer every proper prayer. Such promises He always fulfills. The Scriptures virtually abound with illustrations of the rewarded prayer.

Thus Abraham petitions the Lord for a son: God hears his prayer and, despite the great age of the patriarch and of his wife, gives him a son. Jacob, on his journey to Laban, beseeches Jehovah for help and protection: his prayer is granted with the result that God blesses him visibly during his sojourn of twenty years in the home of Laban, preserves him from Esau's intended vengeance, and finally returns him safe and enriched to his childhood home.

Again, in answer to Joshua's plea the sun stands still upon Gibeon and the moon in the valley of Ajalon until the Israelites complete their defeat of the Amorites. Elijah prays fervently that no rain may fall, and for three years and six months, James writes, no rain fell. Later he climbs Mt. Carmel to ask that the windows of the heavens may be opened to let down their contents to drench the parched earth: in response to his prayer the clouds appear and the rain pours down. King Hezekiah, praying importunately, is delivered from Sennacherib's hosts and is spared from death for an additional fifteen years. Even in the lions' den the Lord hears Daniel's prayer and stays the mouths and claws of the ferocious beasts.

Likewise in the New Testament the poor, the lame, the crippled, the blind, and the lepers who implore the Savior's blessing are healed. Particularly do we note that the congregation at Jerusalem through prayer succeeds in freeing Peter from prison.

Later church history also records remarkable answers of prayer. Monica, the mother of St. Augustine, prayed fervently that God might convert her dissolute and

78

apostate son, who had drifted into the heresy of Mani-chaeism. After some twenty years the Lord mellowed the heart of this proud philosopher living in heathen immorality and made of him one of the foremost of the Latin church fathers.

Several incidents drawn from Luther's life also bear witness to the fact that prayer is answered. On one occasion during the sessions of the Diet of Augsburg in 1530 Luther went to his room and began to pray earnestly and fervently. Shortly thereafter he appeared again and joyfully exclaimed: *"Vicimus,"* that is, "We have conquered." Afterward it was learned that at that identical hour the Diet had adopted the resolution that no harm should be done the adherents of Luther.

On another occasion Philip Melanchthon, Luther's close friend and co-worker, was lying at the point of death in Weimar. Luther at that time was 150 miles distant. Hearing of Melanchthon's severe illness, Luther hurried to his bedside. Having arrived there, he fell on his knees and, with his face turned toward the win-dow, began to wrestle with God in a prayer which lasted for more than an hour. Thereupon he went to the bedside of Melanchthon, who apparently was draw-ing his last breath, took him by the hand, and asked him to be of good cheer and to partake of food. Im-mediately Melanchthon grew better and was speedily restored to health. Later he remarked: "I would have died had I not been torn away from death by Luther's arrival." On two other occasions Luther's prayers for persons apparently at the door of death were answered, so that Luther later could say: "I have restored our Philip [Melanchthon] and my Kate and Mr. Myconius from death by prayer."

A most remarkable story concerning God's answer to a father's prayer is told of Philip Jacob Spener, the so-called Father of Pietism. "Spener, born in 1635 in Upper Alsace, had a very brilliant but very corrupt and incorrigible son. All the kind warnings of his father had no effect on him. Then one day this son became seriously ill and for weeks was confined to his bed. Most of the time he was lying in deep silence, but internally he seemed greatly moved. One day he frantically arose from his bed and exclaimed with a loud voice, 'The prayers of my father are surrounding me like mountains.' From that time on an improvement in his condition set in, and the pious father was granted the joy of seeing his son not only restored to the Christian faith but also promoted to a high station in life." (*Concordia Pulpit*, VII, 312)

Help has occasionally come in marvelous fashion to men in their hour of need, as the illustration of Samuel F. B. Morse, inventor of the telegraph, well demonstrates. Although the recipient of many decorations and awards in recognition of his scientific achievements, Dr. Morse readily acknowledged the power of prayer. When an acquaintance once asked him in the university library, "What do you do, Professor Morse, when in the laboratory experiments you come to a stand, not knowing what to do next?" The humble inventor replied, "I may answer you in confidence. Whenever I could not see my way clearly, I prayed for more light" (Maier, *Winged Words for Christ*, p. 223). So we also, when in need of help and enlightenment amidst the perplexing problems of life, should take our refuge to the Lord in humble prayer.

Another story which teaches us how God gives us strength in answer to prayer in the hour of need is told of the Venerable Bede, father of English history, as he was working on the translation of the four Gospels into the Anglo-Saxon language immediately before his death. In his last hours he had come to the concluding chapters of St. John, and it was Bede's one hope that God would spare him long enough to finish the translation. With his end rapidly approaching, he summoned the scribes for the last time and dictated his translation with feverish speed. The quill pens flew across the parchment, the twentieth chapter of the last Gospel was finished, and his voice broke, but he breathed a prayer to God for strength. One of the sorrowing disciples whispered into his ear, "Dearest master, there is yet one chapter wanting. Will the trouble be too severe?" The dying servant of God replied slowly, "Trouble? There is none. Take your pen, prepare your parchment, and write fast." With amazing, God-given strength he continued to dictate for some time uninterruptedly; but finally, overcome by the exertion, he fell back exhausted. Once more the disciple approached him and, with tears coursing down his cheeks, whispered, "Dearest master, there is yet one sentence unwritten." After a short struggle Adam Bede gasped in faltering tone, "Write quickly." The last verse was completed, his prayer had been answered, and — as a happy smile illumined the countenance of the venerable prophet — he thanked God and exclaimed, "It is finished!" A few moments later he died. Thus God will help his servants in their hour of great physical or spiritual need if they will cry to Him for help in Jesus' name.

Many other stories have been related, particularly of experiences in the mission fields, concerning the wonderful and mysterious manner in which God has answered the prayers of His servants. Repeatedly missionaries have reported that God has provided for their material wants from the most unexpected sources. Although they have made personal sacrifices in leaving behind relatives and friends, our workers in foreign fields write that their experiences often reveal to them the high privilege that is theirs in witnessing to Christ among the heathen. Frequently the Lord has granted remarkable results from the preaching of His Gospel in large baptismal classes and in other unusual accessions to the ranks of the believers.

Because of God's command, the precious promises of Scripture regarding prayer, and the remarkable examples of answered prayers we should be moved to come eagerly to the Lord in prayer. God hears prayer. Of this there can be no legitimate doubt. God pours out His loving heart before us in order that we in turn may feel encouraged to reveal the secret fears and hopes of our heart to Him in the intimate communion of prayer.

What gracious kindness the Lord reveals to us in prayer! What comfort this privilege to pray should afford us mortals, when we know that our cries for mercy and help in our temporal and spiritual trials rise to the throne of heaven! Oh, if we at all times were mindful of God's glorious promises to bless prayer, there would be absolutely no need to admonish, to cajole, to exhort, to encourage to prayer. Then every distressing care, every unkind thought, every crushing grief could vanish as the morning dew, and instead peace and contentment would reign in our heart.

At this point, however, a warning should be sounded against radical and extremist views of the power of prayer. There are those who would convert prayer into a sort of magic, such as the Christian Scientists, who base their false claims for their pseudoscientific art of healing on James 5:14: "Is any sick among you? Let him call the elders of the church, and let them pray over him, anointing him with oil in the name of the Lord." However, this verse by no means justifies the method used by Christian Scientists, according to which in times of sickness the practitioner is called to convince the patient by mental suggestion and oral argument that the sickness is basically a mental aberration or fault. Rather Christians reduce the advice of the apostle to practice when they in the event of sickness call the pastor to come to pray for them.

Another abuse of prayer is practiced by such radical sects as "divine healers," professional faith-curists, and the like, who claim by their prayers to cure all sorts of physical disorders. In order to clothe their practice with apparent Biblical sanction, some of them will refer to Mark 16:17-20, "And these signs shall follow them that believe . . . they shall lay hands on the sick, and they shall recover. . . . And they went forth and preached everywhere, the Lord working with them and confirming the Word with signs following." But in this passage we find no Scriptural warrant for the contention that faith, especially an erring, fanatical faith, working through prayer will always be able to heal, provided only that the patient have confidence in the healer. Rather, according to 1 John 5:14, only when "we ask anything according to His will, He heareth us." Furthermore, Mark 16:20 does not state that the Lord *will confirm* the Word with signs following in every age, but that the Lord at that time *confirmed* the Word with signs for the benefit of that and every age, including our own. Here also apply all those passages which warn against miracle-mindedness, such as John 4:48, 1 Corinthians 1:22; 12:29-31. Therefore all such "divine healing" efforts are an abuse of prayer which all sincere Christians will spurn.

Although extremists have entertained erroneous notions concerning the supposed magical power of prayer and have abused prayer in their mistaken concepts, *prayer does change things.* As Sören Kierkegaard observed, "Prayer does not change God but changes him who prays." It does something to the petitioner as well as for him. Prayer is definitely a character builder. It is this particular phase of prayer life which should engage our attention for a moment in passing.

Since prayer is the communion of the believing heart with the true God, it follows that prayer will also have a pronounced effect on the character of the individual who prays. Communion with the Lord in prayer helps human character to develop in the direction God would have it grow. Many a Christian personality has fallen short of its promise and has become dwarfed and warped because of its failure to keep in touch with God through His Word and prayer.

Prayer, rightly used, requires self-discipline. In true prayer the Christian must recognize the overruling will of God, must bring his own will into conformity with the purposes of the Almighty concerning him, must check his personal pride and ambitions, and merge his personality with Him in whom we "live and move and have our being."

Prayer also affects human character since it is essentially a process of Christian education. Education is not synonymous with instruction. Education means growth, development, training for life. In this sense Christian prayer is education because it exercises and develops the powers of the soul, controls the will, subordinates self to God, and presents the entire Christian personality through Christ to the Lord of heaven and earth for guidance, help, and service.

Moreover, the practice of fervent prayer strengthens the mind by sustained thought as the Christian wrestles with his God. Habitual prayer invigorates the believer's will and develops his moral life by projecting the Christian petitioner into the celestial atmosphere inhabited by Him who answers prayer. By bringing the suppliant into the felt presence of God, true prayer produces a sense of sinfulness in the Christian and instills a becoming humility of mind which expresses itself in submission of the will to Him who knows all and who "hath done all things well." Such intimate communion with God in prayer produces peace, hope, joy, spiritual power, and confidence.

XI

Prayer Needs Today

THE INCENTIVE to prayer which the average man probably feels most quickly and keenly is that furnished by pressing need, compelling necessity. As the little child instinctively hurries to its parents when it is in trouble, so the Christian is impelled to approach his heavenly Father when confronted by some urgent material or spiritual want.

Imperative material or physical needs serve to drive men to God. Such are, as Luther enumerates them in his explanation of the Fourth Petition: "food, drink, clothing, shoes, house, home, field, cattle, money, goods" — all of which are necessary for the daily sustenance of our life and that of the members of our family. Furthermore, we cannot expect peace and happiness to flourish within our home without "a pious spouse, pious children, pious servants." Again, for our own welfare and that of every citizen of our far-flung country, "good government" is necessary. "Good weather" is required in order that crops may be planted, mature, and be harvested and that fruits may blossom and ripen. Finally, "peace, health, discipline, honor, good friends, faithful neighbors," and similar blessings are indispensable necessities for the welfare of our body and life. All these gifts come from God, the Author and Giver of all good gifts.

And even though we should lack none of them we ought nonetheless pray for them in order that we may receive them with thanksgiving.

In addition to the material wants just enumerated there are certain evils, peculiarly characteristic of our modern times, which incite us to seek the Lord in prayer. In the realm of nature of late there have been, for instance, droughts which have shriveled and scorched promising crops; dust storms that have carried away the fertile topsoil from millions of western acres, virtually reducing them to desert wastes; locust plagues that have wiped out not only crops but every verdant substance overnight, leaving the earth bare of all vegetation; floods that have wreaked untold havoc in loss of property and life with their turbid, swirling, devastating torrents; and tornadoes, hurricanes, and earthquakes which have resulted in tremendous losses to real estate and which baffle the mind of scientist and layman alike.

Moreover, black headlines in our daily papers scream the news of wars and threats of wars; of an epidemic of strikes which has spread its contagion into widely separated and greatly differing fields of industrial and commercial activity; of rumors of attempts by communistic, fascistic, and other insurrectional organizations to gain control of national governments; and of multitudinous social, economic, and political problems identified with our modern materialistic age.

And the church, compelled to expand its activities because of a changed social order, finds itself through organizations within itself establishing and supporting institutions of mercy for the care of the mentally and physically underprivileged or institutions of learning for the education of its teachers and lay people. All such modern evils and problems should become the burden of Christian prayer.

However, even more than material exigencies should spiritual needs incite to prayer, for spiritual necessities by their very nature are imperatively required for our welfare. To possess *Word* and *sacrament* in their truth and purity is more urgent even than food and drink for the body. Without *faith* we could not escape eternal damnation. If the Lord would not *strengthen* and *protect* us in the true faith against our spiritual enemies, Satan, the world, and our sinful flesh, we should soon be lost. We daily sin much and consequently need *forgiveness* of all our sins. If the Holy Spirit does not dwell within our hearts, we lack peace, comfort, the assurance of the adoption as children of God, and strength for spiritual renewal and Christian warfare.

Moreover, our prayers should embrace the church's educational institutions which have been established to prepare Christian laymen, pastors, and teachers for work in the Kingdom in order to insure the preservation and continued progress of the Church Militant. If God does not bless this phase of the church's work, if He does not assist in the constant battle which must be waged against every invasion by false doctrine and materialism, the cause of the church is soon lost.

But in the sphere of spiritual things there are certain evils and problems to be identified particularly with twentieth-century life. Also these should be the burden of the Christian's prayer. Such are, among others, liberalism and unionism working hand in hand to weaken and undermine the foundations of the church; the modern evils of delinquency, vice, and crime fed largely by sensual and vicious programs on radio, television, screen, and stage and by the horror stories and pictures featured in today's magazines and comic strips; the problems associated with certain types of the dance; the evils of drink; the challenge of the unconverted, the lack of funds and missionaries, and other mission problems which confront the church more insistently today than at any other time in its history.

Certainly no one dare deny that these are critical times. But desperate need inclines the Christian to prayer. This is an axiomatic truth. "Sinking times are praying times with the Lord's servants. When Peter began to sink on his journey, his danger made him a suppliant. The fox hies to his hole for protection; the bird flies to the woods for shelter; and even so the tried believer hastens to the mercy-seat for safety. Heaven's great harbor of refuge is All-prayer; thousands of weather-beaten vessels have found a haven there, and the moment a storm comes on, it is wise for us to make for it with all sail." (Spurgeon, quoted in *Concordia Pulpit*, VII, 310)

Why, then, should we for a moment hesitate to carry our urgent material and spiritual needs to the Lord in fervent, persevering prayer? Let us be up and active in prayer while it is day, ere the night comes when it shall be too late to pray.

As an illustration, let us picture to ourselves this hypothetical situation with regard to missions: If every individual Christian would importune God in unremitting prayer for the conversion of the heathen, missions both at home and abroad would make such rapid strides forward as to require vast increases in funds and personnel; and these, too, would be forthcoming if we would sincerely desire and fervently pray and earnestly

89

work for the spreading of His kingdom. In this regard our Lord Himself bids us: "Pray ye therefore the Lord of the harvest that He will send forth laborers into His harvest" (Matthew 9:38). Realizing this, let us persevere and not grow faint in prayer.

Prayer has power. It is a means by which God is influenced in His divine decrees and in His regulation of the affairs of the universe. Prayer, it has been said, moves the Hand that moves the world. Prayer has also been likened to the "shorting" of a charged battery. When the negative and the positive pole of a battery are brought into contact with each other by means of some conducting agent, a spark of fire is given off. When man's desperate need is brought face to face with God's power and mercy in believing prayer, something notable results. Where the raging sea and the lowering sky meet there is a waterspout. God hears the Christian's prayer and answers it in His way.

But prayer has its own reward in another respect. It has been said that prayer has a reflex action, that it is a natural and salutary exercise of the mind and soul. It does one good to pray. When someone goes with a sincere heart to God, does he ever return without some comfort, peace, satisfaction, or relief? He may hear no voice, no discernible sounds in the air, see no visions, experience no transcending thrill in body or soul, yet somehow there comes in answer to prayer a peaceful quiet that slips into the soul, something that lifts the crushing burden from the shoulder, that refreshes and quickens the fainting heart, that converts despondency and despair into courage and joyful confidence and hope. Prayer actually changes things. More important, it changes the one who prays.

Prayer has been variously styled by authors as "the 'harp of David' before which the Evil One must flee; 'Jacob's Ladder,' which leads from earth to heaven; the 'golden chain' which binds us to God; the 'jawbone of Samson' with which we can vanquish our foes; the 'rod of Moses' with which we are able to smite the rock and fetch forth water; 'the key to the heavenly vaults'; the 'ship' in which we shall be gallantly and safely carried through storm and waves" (Central District *Proceedings*, 1924, p. 29). It is one of the most blessed privileges which we mortals possess in this critical age; that we may approach our heavenly Father directly, unbosom ourselves to Him as we dare not even to our most intimate earthly friend, and as a result find comfort, reassurance, and strength.

Why is it that some complain that their prayers are not answered? An excellent answer is supplied in *A Short Explanation of Luther's Small Catechism* (pp. 149, 150): "God has not promised to answer prayers which are not offered in faith and with confidence; which ask for foolish and hurtful things; which prescribe to God the time when He should help and the manner in which He should help," and: "Christians sometimes feel that their . . . prayers are not answered because in the hour of trial they do not at once observe the helping hand of God."

Such unfortunate people either have not been guided by the Scriptural specifications in prayer or have been blinded by their own afflictions to God's answer of their prayer. Every proper prayer is answered. Let us therefore not permit tribulations to act as hindrances or barriers to prayer. Luther writes: "We should learn the fine art of making the very thoughts which would disturb us and keep us from prayer incite us the more to it, as we read of the blind man in the Gospel, who, the more he was told to hold his peace, cried the louder, 'Have mercy on me, O Lord.'" May the Lord likewise hear us as we cry to Him amidst the evils and needs of our critical times.

XII

GRATITUDE AND PRAYER

WHEN the Lord *has* answered prayer, when at His time and in His way He has delivered us from the evils or needs which have driven us to Him, we should not neglect to prove our gratitude by lifting a tribute of thanks and praise to His throne.

Ingratitude is characteristic of mankind. Man habitually neglects to tender thanks for the blessings he has received at the hand of his Creator. But the Christian by the grace of God seeks to rid himself of the spirit of thanklessness and habitually includes the element of thanks and praise in his act of communion with God.

The Christian finds abundant cause for praise in the wonders of God. There are, first of all, the wonders of creation that act as an incentive to the prayer of praise. Luther mentions a few of these marvels in his summary of the grandeur of the work of creation, contained in the explanation of the First Article. God has given us "body and soul, eyes, ears, and all our members, our reason, and all our senses," to mention a few of the material gifts with which God has endowed every human being.

Let us stop for a moment to marvel at God's creation, which reveals His infinite love toward mankind in that

He has bestowed innumerable gifts upon every individual of the more than two and one-half billion human beings who today populate the earth. Every earth-born man is endowed with a body composed of billions of cells which are constantly changing, never static, either growing more vibrant with life or else chilling in the grip of advancing death. With the psalmist we are moved to say: "Marvelous are Thy works, and that my soul knoweth right well." (Psalm 139:14)

Truly marvelous is the body which we possess. In order to stamp this conviction more indelibly upon our minds, let us study the function of one organ of the body, the eye, in its relation to the organs of speech. We fix the eye, for instance, on some tree before us. The image of the tree is immediately pictured on the mirror of the eye as on a photographic plate and is transmitted to the brain with the speed of lightning. And more quickly than one may describe with words, the mind comprehends the scene which the eye flashes to it, selects from it the object of the tree, reaches a decision, and transmits to tongue and lips the message to emit the sound which designates the object which the eye beholds. No sooner is this message received by the tongue and lips than they act and utter the word "tree."

Surely this functioning of the human eye is most marvelous. The memory which has stored away thousands of images in its recesses immediately recognizes the object, reason arrives at a correct decision, and the will sends to the tongue and lips an impulse which is forthwith obeyed. This marvel of the human mind is repeated innumerable times each day, not only within the experience of one individual but in the lives of each of the two and one-half billion inhabitants of the world who enjoy the privilege of sight.

Furthermore, consider the convenient position of the eye, so situated in the skull that it may readily behold whatever the human being faces; it is in close proximity to the brain, protected by the surrounding bone structure of the skull, and shielded by eyelids which shut out blinding light and by sensitive eyelashes which warn of danger from objects approaching too closely.

As it is with the eye, so also with the remaining organs of the body. Surely, we cannot refrain from joining with David in his prayer of thanks: "I will praise Thee, for I am fearfully and wonderfully made" (Psalm 139:14). Indeed, as we deduce from the eye, the human being is marvelously and wonderfully created.

With this same eye man may look about him in the world and behold the handiwork of God in nature. God could have created everything in one indistinguishable, colorless mass. But instead, he created the green grass, the blue sky, the golden sunset, the crimson sunrise, the glistening dewdrops, the blossoming trees, plants, and flowers in all the brilliant hues of the rainbow. We who are blessed with the gift of sight are privileged to view these beauties of nature as they are affected by the various seasons of the year and by varying degrees of intensity of light, a picture of ever-changing, lavish, riotous color which no artist can duplicate from his imagination without the assistance of the original itself. In addition, we are privileged to behold the mountains in their constantly changing hues, and the sea, whose fascinating colors defy efforts of reproduction by the artist's brush because their shades change with each passing cloud, each subsequent bath of sunlight, and each whitecapped or lazily undulating wave. Such are the wonders of nature. We exclaim with the poet:

If God has made this world so fair,
Where sin and death abound,
How wonderful, beyond compare,
Will Paradise be found!

Into His creation God has placed creatures in multitudinous quantities and multifarious forms. Whoever has taken an excursion aboard the glass-bottom boats at Catalina Island off the coast of California, or at Silver Springs, Florida, has been amazed at the wonders of the ocean floor with its shimmering shadows, its undulating forests of sea vegetation, and its myriads of brilliant-hued fishes. The ocean bed is replete with animal and vegetative life. And as everything at the bottom of the sea is stirring with life, so the air is filled with birds and insects in great number and in variegated color.

When we think of all these wonders of nature and creation, we cannot escape an overwhelming admiration for the marvels of God, who not only has created them but continues to produce them according to kind and to preserve them. Truly marvelous are the works of God in the realm of nature. This conviction should lead us to express our admiration in prayers of praise.

But we are impelled to praise God not only for the wonders of His divine omnipotence in material things but also for the wonders of His mercy in the realm of spiritual things — mercy which hails from the foundation of the world, even from eternity. These wonders of God's mercy are described in Luther's explanation of the Second and the Third Article of the Apostles' Creed. Even there all things are not recounted which God does

96

for the individual Christian — how He provides for the believer in weal and woe, seeks and saves, directs and upholds, lifts up and blesses. Every Christian who has experienced the wonders of justification and sanctification must out of a spirit of gratitude thank and praise God.

If we were permitted to page through God's record of the sins of mankind, what tragedies of sullen apostasy and pernicious wickedness would unfold before our eyes! We would be astounded by the enduring forbearance, by the infinite love, and by the pardoning mercy of a gracious God, who sent His precious, only-born Son into the world to suffer and die for condemned, sin-stricken mankind. As we read of the ravings and persecutions of a Saul against the disciples of the Lord or of the perverse waywardness of an Augustine, we marvel at the grace of God which conquered their spirits and melted their hearts.

And if we review the impact of God's love upon our own refractory spirits, we are compelled to rejoice with David and say: "Bless the Lord, O my soul, and all that is within me, bless His holy name. Bless the Lord, O my soul, and forget not all His benefits, who forgiveth all thine iniquities, who healeth all thy diseases, who redeemeth thy life from destruction, who crowneth thee with loving-kindness and tender mercies" (Psalm 103: 1-4). Yes, the wonders of God both in the realm of material and of spiritual things *must* lead us to thank and praise Him in prayer.

XIII

Answer Problems of Prayer

THERE IS scarcely a Christian, be he ever so devout, who in extreme adversity has not had some question or doubt concerning God's answer to his prayer. He prays, prays fervently, in Jesus' name, trusting in God's promises; he is certain that his request is not contrary to the will of the Lord. Yet there seems to be no answer. God appears deaf to his pleas, the heavens as unyielding as brass. At other times the answer, if it does come, is long delayed. In still other instances the results, if they constitute heaven's reply to the petition, are strangely different from what the prayer requested. Such situations pose more or less acute problems for anyone who prays.

In all such cases, however, we should bear in mind that we are not by any means the most qualified judge of what is the proper answer to our prayer. Perhaps in a given instance what seemed to be a denial of our request was the best answer.

Certainly the most fervent prayer recorded in Scripture was our Redeemer's plea, made with blood and sweat in the Garden of Gethsemane, that the heavenly Father would remove from Him the cup of His suffering for mankind's transgressions. To this petition the Suffering Servant readily added the qualification that His Father's will be done. Nevertheless, the Father denied

His Son's request for release from the agony and death required for our redemption when He required Jesus to drain that cup to its bitterest dregs that the price of sin be paid in full.

Now, did not God answer Jesus' prayer? Most assuredly. The heavenly Father's decision that His Son must face man's scorn, abuse, and torture, even death on the accursed cross, was a much more complete and satisfactory answer to the Savior's prayer than if the cup had been permitted to pass from His trembling hand without His drinking it. Our Lord's suffering and death on our behalf won for Him the glory of being mankind's Redeemer, our Mediator in time, the Judge of the world at the end of time, and the King of heaven for endless time.

The prayers of even the best-intentioned of God's loving children are sometimes ignorant and foolish. The Christian becomes overeager in his zeal for good or impatient with his cross. Blinded by tears, bewildered by problems, frustrated by adversity, he comes to Him whose wisdom probes the deepest mystery with a plea that on the surface appears good but in the wisdom of the all-knowing God would be unwise, even tragic. So desperate at times is his supplication that he may even request the Almighty to suspend the laws of nature and produce a state of anarchy to satisfy a desire on which he has set his heart and which with undoubting faith he is sure God will give him. To such a pathetic view of prayer can extremity sometimes reduce even the informed believer.

God, however, knows better than we. He is a God of love. His love embraces particularly the individual. But in His wisdom the Lord views the individual in his

99

relation to the world, the part as a segment of the whole, and time in terms of eternity. With eternal patience and with infinite wisdom the Lord designs and executes all things so that our destinies are interwoven with His vast and incomprehensible pattern. The end result is that sometimes the answer we seek in prayer does not come, and does not come because something better has been substituted, something that will more truly serve God's wise and loving providential purposes concerning us. We may not always understand, but this we should surely know, that God's ways are best and that He always leads us in the proper path.

> He leadeth me.
> In pastures green? No, not always.
> Sometimes He who knoweth best
> In kindness leadeth me in weary ways
> Where heavy shadows be;
> Out of the sunshine warm and soft and bright,
> Out of the sunshine into darkest night.
> I oft would yield to sorrow and to fright
> Only for this: I know He holds my hand.
> So, whether led in green or desert land,
> I trust, although I cannot understand.
>
> He leadeth me.
> Beside still waters? No, not always so.
> Ofttimes the heavy tempests round me blow.
> And o'er my soul the waves and billows go.
> But when the storm beats wildest and I cry
> Aloud for help, the Master standeth by
> And whispers to my soul: "Lo, it is I."
> Above the tempest wild I hear Him say:
> "Beyond the darkness lies the perfect day;
> In every path of thine I lead the way."

So whether on the hilltops high and fair
I dwell, or in the sunless valleys, where
The shadows lie — what matter? He is there.
And more than this; where'er the pathway lead,
He gives to me no helpless, broken reed,
But His own hand, sufficient for my need.
So where He leads me I can safely go.
And in the blest hereafter I shall know
Why in His wisdom He hath led me so.

Tract No. 142, Book Mission of the ELC

Although we frequently are unable to explain why our prayers are not answered, this is not necessarily or always true. Sometimes our requests are denied because we ask for something harmful. Wisdom and experience teach that we should never be at cross purposes with our God. God knows that we occasionally in ignorance ask for things that do not promote our spiritual welfare. Accordingly, He in our best interest denies our petition.

Again, sometimes our petition is denied in order that we may receive a higher and better blessing. The apostle Paul repeatedly and earnestly requested the removal of a "thorn" from his flesh, but his gracious heavenly Father denied his prayer so that by means of this infirmity he might draw nearer to God and through more intimate communion with Him might experience richer joy and happiness than any physical relief the granting of his wish might have brought him. Our experience with prayer can be the same. God give us grace to recognize the wisdom of His ways.

And again, our prayer may be denied because it is not in harmony with God's will concerning us. As members of the family of heaven by faith in Christ, we may be sure that whatever happens in response to

101

our prayers is for our welfare. If the Lord denies a request because in His omniscience He sees that it would result in some spiritual harm to us or because it would not fit into the Almighty's scheme of things for His kingdom at large, we cheerfully ought to submit to His will and accept His verdict.

In exceptional cases it happens that we do not realize that prayer has been answered. Under the strain of suffering or stress of tensions or with the numbness of bereavement and loss, it may occasionally come to pass that we are so confused and bewildered that reason no longer functions normally and we are not aware of God's answer to our prayer. Upon return to a calmer state we may suddenly behold how the Lord has granted our wish, perhaps in a mysterious way. As with the disciples on the road to Emmaus, in our grief and emotional disturbance our "eyes were held." Many times a strong faith is required to discern God's answer to prayer.

Actually there is no such thing as unanswered prayer, provided all conditions for proper prayer are met. Proper prayer is always answered in some manner and at some time. God is not like an irresponsible man who permits telephone calls to go unanswered or mail to be unacknowledged. The promise of the Lord is: "And it shall come to pass that, before they call, I will answer; and while they are yet speaking, I will hear" (Isaiah 65:24). Also: "He shall call upon Me, and I will answer him" (Psalm 91:15). Nowhere in Scripture is there a record of an unanswered prayer by a believing child of God. There are instances of requests in prayer being denied, but always such petitions were granted in a higher and better way than originally placed.

Sometimes the answer to prayer is delayed. If the request made in the prayer seems to be legitimate, the delay may puzzle the devout suppliant. Although human beings may not comprehend the cause for the delay, the Lord always has an excellent reason. When His purposes have been achieved, the answer to prayer will at once be forthcoming. Therefore the praying Christian must learn to wait patiently upon the Lord.

Perhaps the answer to prayer is delayed for the sake of spiritual discipline. We must learn patience, humility, and hope. Prolonged suffering can under God develop Christian character. Delayed answer to prayer may strengthen faith through exercise, increase the fervency of prayer, promote greater appreciation of blessings, and intensify communion with the Lord.

The answer to prayer may be delayed because of a faulty attitude of the petitioner. Some presume to dictate to the Lord the time and place for the fulfillment of requests. Such presumption ignores the Christian's relationship to God as one of suppliant to his benefactor, of child to his parent. As such, the child of God is in no position to dictate terms. The decision when the answer is to come, where it is to be supplied, and what form it is to take is a matter entirely for our God to determine. Impatience with God is the meanest type of distrust. Such spiritual faults must be corrected by our heavenly Father's discipline before He grants an answer to our prayer.

Sometimes the answer to prayer is delayed because the request is not according to the will of God, at least not for the time being. The Syrophoenician woman cried after Jesus, imploring help for her daughter, but our Lord did not grant her request until the greatness of her faith demonstrated itself in the fervency and persistence of her prayer. Mary and Martha implored the Master to come at once to heal Lazarus' illness, but He delayed His arrival until the brother of the Bethany sisters had been buried for four days, in order to teach Mary and Martha patience, and through the resurrection of Lazarus the great truth of Christ's power over death and the reality of the resurrection of the body at the Last Day. So the answer to our prayer may be delayed until God's purposes in and for us have developed.

Unanswered yet, the prayer your lips have pleaded
In agony of heart these many years?
Does faith begin to fail? Is hope departing,
And think you all in vain those falling tears?
Say not the Father hath not heard your prayer;
You shall have your desire sometime, somewhere.

Unanswered yet? Nay, do not say ungranted;
Perhaps your part is not yet wholly done;
The work began when first your prayer was uttered,
And God will finish what He has begun.
If you will keep the incense burning there,
His glory you will see sometime, somewhere.

— Ophelia Guyon Browning

A prayer is not unanswered simply because it was not answered as we had requested or expected. Sometimes God sees fit to grant a *different answer,* an answer we as loving children of God can be certain is far better and nobler than anything we might have conceived. One day, when the mysteries of life have been unraveled and in the light of eternity we can see more clearly how "goodness and mercy have followed us all the days of our life," we shall behold in all their fullness the glory and wisdom of our God in His answers to our prayers.

Thus we pray for material blessings: God answers with spiritual benefits. We ask to be freed from some burden: God answers with strength and patience to bear it. We desire to be spared trial and tribulation: God answers with courage and perseverance to endure to a victorious end. God's overruling purpose for His children is the growth of the Christian personality in whom faith, hope, courage, love, patience, and perseverance are developed to their highest capacities. The fulfillment of this purpose of God in our lives would be our greatest blessing.

The Christian who prays for God's help and finds himself growing stronger and more determined in the face of multiplied reverses, has been answered even though he doesn't know it. The Christian who prays for patience and perseverance though God seems to be deaf or dead, has been answered even if he is not aware of it. Meanwhile faith has grown stronger, love has become intensified, hunger and thirst after righteousness has increased, patience has developed, and courage has taken deeper root. If in the end the direct answer to prayer should also come, the Christian will discover that the direct and visible gift is not as valuable as the blessings which God has bestowed in the process. Sooner or later we must learn that God knows best.

XIV

Objections to Prayer

ADMITTEDLY there are very real and great difficulties connected with the rationale of prayer. This is not surprising when one realizes that in the act of prayer the mystery of man meets the mystery of God. Many physiological and psychological factors in man are still a mystery to science, and philosophy can only speculate concerning them. When these mysterious influences that affect the being and actions of man are compounded with the profound and inscrutable mystery surrounding the personality and will of God, the puny mind of man must quite naturally be confounded. Nevertheless, from the multitude of objections that have been raised to prayer we shall abstract two groups of arguments, the scientific and the philosophical, as most pertinent to the Christian concept of prayer.

From the scientific point of view there is no objection to the generally accepted fact that the act of prayer in itself has some reflex benefit on the soul of the person who prays. Science contends, however, that answered prayer involves a violation of the laws of nature. Scientists contend that it is irrational to expect prayer to influence the inflexible rules governing the operation of our universe. Cosmic law is unconcerned with the problems of puny man; it is altogether amoral and impersonal. It is positively preposterous to expect the

Almighty to side-track the through traffic of the world to give the right of way to a local freight train carrying the requests of some individual's prayer. At least so the intellectuals reason.

Specifically, physical science argues: Everywhere there is evidence of absolute, fixed law, which governs the universe and controls the affairs of men according to precise, inflexible regulations. Accordingly, how can anyone reasonably expect prayer to God — if there be a God — to interrupt or suspend basic natural law in order to supply the needs or gratify the wish of some individual?

Generations ago — so the argument runs — before the age of scientific research, ignorance of the existence of fixed laws governing all of nature led men to attribute what seemed to be caprice at work in the world to the will of God or to some "Supreme Intelligence." Not comprehending the operation of the universe, man quite naturally prayed to some higher being for rain and sunshine, health and abundant crops, peace and protection. But now that science has discovered, defined, and classified the basic laws of nature it is no longer reasonable to speak of the power of prayer.

Intelligent people know that rain or sunshine are determined by atmospheric conditions governed by certain meteorological laws. Life and health are dependent on the operation of certain physiological laws which will inevitably determine when and how a man will die. To speak of health and sickness, peace and war, prosperity and poverty as being dependent on the will of God, who will grant or withdraw them according to His pleasure, is therefore utterly unscientific and unintelligent. Such views reflect gross ignorance on the part of a Christian who prays. In substance such is the argument of many scientists.

But the conflict between the views of some scientists and the pronouncements of Biblical theology regarding prayer lies basically in a definition of what constitutes natural law. If by a law of nature we mean some self-existent and self-determining invisible force that is both blind and inflexible, then we have ruled God out of existence. Then we have a fatalistic concept of life. Then man is the mere pawn of blind and irresponsible force. Then prayer is futile.

If, however, by a law of nature we mean a basic principle which accounts for the observable regularity and uniformity with which God controls and operates the universe, "then in our contact with law we are dealing, not with a brutal, unintelligent, unconquerable force but with the free will of an intelligent and moral Artist, who works, in His perfect freedom, with sustained and beautiful symmetry" (James Hastings, *The Christian Doctrine of Prayer*, p. 226). If we accept the latter definition of a law of nature, why then should it be absurd to ask the Almighty to suspend some law altogether or to speed its operation? Certainly then our God can be trusted to grant or refuse our prayer as seems best to Him, as determined by His perfect wisdom and infinite love. Then it becomes clear that He can modify the operation of some lower law in favor of some higher principle.

As a matter of fact, all of us are constantly interfering (properly understood) with the natural functions of the physical order in which we live. Every action on our part brings about an interplay of forces, each of which is regulated by natural law. In so doing we do not alter a law of nature. We actually alter the operation of forces each of which is regulated by law. Thus it is a law of nature that fire burns, and when I light some inflammable material, it will burst into flame. But when I pour water on that flame, it is extinguished. In so doing I have altered no law of nature, but I have brought about an interaction of forces, each controlled by laws, that has resulted in change. In that sense man can and constantly does interfere with the forces of nature and by such interference achieves change.

What is true of man is true in a much higher sense of God. If man can alter the course of natural forces, most certainly God, with whom nothing is impossible and who is the Supreme Intelligence who has created and operates these forces, can, in answer to prayer, change, modify, suspend, and expedite the operation of natural forces.

If by a miracle we mean a departure from what according to the laws of nature would have been God's expected mode of operation in the universe, then the answer to prayer is always a miracle. For every true answer to prayer disturbs the normal operation of existing laws to secure the intervention of a higher law. Therefore the difference between raising a dead person in answer to prayer and granting a slight wish, likewise in answer to prayer, is merely a difference of degree. Thank God for the miraculous power of prayer!

In the realm of philosophical objections to prayer, there is, first of all, the argument of man's self-sufficiency. Some philosophers point out that man is equipped with remarkable natural powers, talents, and capacities, many of which continue undiscovered or undeveloped throughout life. If the human being would make the fullest use of his physical, intellectual, moral, psychological, and spiritual endowments, he would not need the support of prayer.

But this supposed incompatibility of human self-sufficiency with prayer is based on the false assumption that prayer is to be used alone. There are possibly some fanatics who do not call a physician in time of illness but rely solely on the power of prayer for a cure. If so, they misunderstand Scripture, which offers no promise to those who wilfully neglect ordinary means. The old Latin proverb *Ora et labora* truly expresses the Christian philosophy of prayer, "Pray and work." Pray that God may bless your work. Labor lest your prayer put God on trial. "Thou shalt not tempt the Lord thy God," Jesus warned Satan. (Matthew 4:7)

Again, there are times when human effort alone is powerless. A loved one is at the point of death. Medical science has exhausted its efforts. Obviously this is the time when prayer alone can help. Even if the petition for the recovery of the stricken individual is not granted, because it is not in harmony with the sovereign, loving will of the heavenly Father, a prayer that God would receive the departing soul and comfort the bereaved family would be most helpful under the circumstances.

Another philosophical objection to prayer is that frequently it involves a conflict of interests among men and nations. What one individual requests interferes with the concerns of another. During the first two world wars Americans prayed for victory over the Germans, Germans prayed for the success of their armed forces against the Allies. One prays for rain, another for sunshine on the same day for the same general area. How can God be expected to answer prayers representing such conflicting interests?

110

The answer to this objection is that every Christian prayer for such material blessings is either tacitly or expressly conditioned on the will of God. Three such conditions are enumerated in the Lord's Prayer: "Hallowed be Thy name. Thy kingdom come. Thy will be done." In the last analysis all three are only one. The true believer, in all his prayers for such blessings as are not necessary for his soul's salvation, should add the condition: "Nevertheless, not my will but Thine be done." The Christian in his prayer must always acknowledge that God knows what is best for him and all of God's children and that God's ways are always right.

Again, some schools of philosophical thought raise the objection to prayer that man is too insignificant to influence the great God in prayer. The reason: when one considers how infinitestimally small man is in comparison with the universe, in which many of the planets are thousands of times larger than the world on which man is a speck, how can one reasonably conclude that man and his needs could even remotely concern the Lord of the universe, who is preoccupied with other vastly more important duties?

The great fault with this objection is that it seeks to compress the infinite into the confines of the finite. Philosophy does God a great injustice in trying to limit His infinite capacities by the faulty comprehension of our petty minds. God cannot be understood or measured in material terms. So far as human reason is concerned God is the ultimate, eternal Mystery. He informs us: "My thoughts are not your thoughts, neither are your ways My ways. For as the heavens are higher than the earth, so are My ways higher than your ways and My thoughts than your thoughts" (Isaiah 55:8, 9). Although philosophy may not be able to comprehend, God assures

111

the Christian that as an individual he is important in the sight of the Lord and that the Ruler of the universe hears his prayer.

In this connection we think of such Scripture passages as: "Are not two sparrows sold for a farthing? And one of them shall not fall on the ground without your Father. But the very hairs of your head are all numbered. Fear ye not, therefore; ye are of more value than many sparrows" (Matthew 10:29-31). "Call upon Me in the day of trouble. I will deliver thee, and thou shalt glorify Me" (Psalm 50:15). "Call unto Me, and I will answer thee and shew thee great and mighty things which thou knowest not" (Jeremiah 33:3). Quite obviously, then, the believer is not the insignificant, forgotten, and neglected atom of the universe that philosophers have pictured him in the sight of his Creator. Rather, every Christian may be sure that every proper prayer is heard and answered.

Then there is the philosophic objection that God's providence is perfect. He knows all. His ways are not merely best but perfect. His wisdom is infinite, absolute. If "prayer moves the Hand that guides the world," they contend, "who are we to grasp the reins from the hands of the all-perfect Ruler of the world? Would it not be presumption on the part of us fallible humans to interfere with God's infallible government of the universe?"

This line of reasoning overlooks the true purpose of prayer. The intent of prayer is not to *inform* God, who knows all things, even the mysteries which scientists and philosophers seek in vain to unravel by human reason. Rather our prayers have as their purpose *communion* with a Lord who in Scripture has bidden us to pray. In our communion with God we are not to inform and teach but to worship and learn. In our prayers we are to be educated in our personal relations with God. We come to God in prayer to acknowledge Him as Giver of every good and perfect gift. In prayer we achieve a clearer realization of our endless need of Him. It is His will that we pray, not merely to receive what we ask — although we must ask that we may receive — but to bring us as children of God to our heavenly Father's knee that we may commune with Him and thereby grow and profit spiritually.

The previous objection dovetails with the last of the philosophical arguments against prayer: that prayer is inconsistent with the truth that *God's will is unchangeable*. Philosophers reason: "Since all things which come to pass are predetermined in God's will, how can prayer change them? Unless the will of God is subject to change, where is there room for prayer in God's scheme of things?"

To this objection, too, there is a convincing answer. Although human reason finds it difficult to reconcile the two facts of God's eternal foreknowledge and the power of prayer, we must not on that account ignore either. On the one hand, we should of all creatures be the most miserable and hopeless if we were to abandon the Scriptural teaching that God's purposes in Christ are interwoven like a golden thread through history and beyond. His purposes of love, which from eternity have determined what shall come to pass, will eventually lead to their intended end. On the other hand, we would drift through life as helpless pawns of fate if we did not believe that our prayers do influence the Almighty, who governs and directs the affairs of the universe.

113

In God's government of the world our prayers have been foreseen and taken into account. God's answers to our petitions are embraced in His eternal decrees. From our point of view it may appear that our prayers have changed God's disposition and will. From God's point of view our prayers were foreseen in all eternity, foreknown, and included in His dispensation. Accordingly it is true, as Scripture plainly teaches: with "the Father of lights" there is in this sense "no variableness, neither shadow of turning"; and yet at the same time it is not inconsistent for us to pray for specific blessings. God performs His work not only in us but also through us, and by our prayers He can and does accomplish His purposes planned before the foundation of the world.

XV

Models of Prayer Life

IN ADDITION to the command and promises of God relating to prayer, also the Scriptural examples of prayer life should incite us to more abundant use of prayer.

It is but natural that when we think of models of prayer life, the Savior's example should immediately suggest itself. When we study the Lord's brief residence among men, as it is recorded in the Scriptures, we are amazed at His intense prayer activity. For instance, on several occasions after addressing the multitudes which followed Him, He went aside upon a mountain to pray. Once He spent the entire night in prayer on a mountain. After the strenuous activity of preaching and performing miracles — instead of resting — He prayed. Again, several times we read that He departed into the wilderness to pray.

The Lord was accustomed to pray whenever He engaged in any extraordinary activity. When He was baptized and entered upon His public ministry, He prayed. Again, when He raised Lazarus from the dead, He thanked His heavenly Father for always hearing His prayers. The night of His betrayal He offered that comprehensive High-priestly Prayer in behalf of His disciples and gave thanks at the institution of the Lord's Supper in the Upper Room at Jerusalem. Arriving in the Garden

115

of Gethsemane that selfsame night, He prayed three times. The next day He uttered two prayers on the cross.

Furthermore, Jesus gave us an illustrious example by praying for all people. Not only did He pray for Himself, for the immediate Twelve, and for the larger circle of His disciples, but He prayed for the little children, for those who would be converted by the disciples, for the entire New Testament church, and even for His bitter enemies.

Moreover, it is instructive to note how the Lord in His prayers distinguished between material and spiritual gifts. While He teaches His disciples to pray for the gift of the Holy Spirit without condition, He in Gethsemane conditions His own prayer with the words, "Nevertheless not My will but Thine be done" (Luke 22:42). That His prayers were fervent and earnest Hebrews 5:7 discloses: "Who in the days of His flesh, when He had offered up prayers and supplications with strong crying and tears unto Him that was able to save Him from death." So Jesus by His blessed example would teach us when, where, and how to pray.

From this divine pattern of perfect prayer life we turn to Old Testament models of prayer. All the great men of God of Old Testament history led prayer lives which to a greater or lesser extent may serve as fitting patterns for all Christians. Among those whose prayer life is described in some detail we find the patriarchs Abraham, Isaac, and Jacob, the prophets Moses, Samuel, Elijah, and Daniel, the priest Ezra, the statesman Nehemiah, and King Solomon.

Numerous prayers of considerable length are also recorded for our diligent study on the pages of the Old Testament. Of these the prayer of Solomon at the dedication of the temple, Hannah's hymn of praise after the birth of Samuel, and the penitential prayers of Daniel, Ezra, and Nehemiah stand out. The petitions of Elijah for drought and later for rain also come to mind.

However, as a human model of prayer life without peer or equal in Old Testament times, David must be our choice. His prayers, which compose the major portion of the Psalter — the greatest prayer book and hymnal ever written — for beauty of expression, for humility of spirit, for sincerity of confession, and for fervency of petition surpass any prayers ever created by a human mind.

If the believer will only take the time to study David's psalms, he will gradually comprehend how vast and varied was the king's prayer activity. David's petitions embrace almost the entire range of human emotions and thoughts. There is scarcely a subject or an occasion for which one cannot find a suitable psalm from the pen of David. Truly he lived a life of prayer.

He could say of his prayer life: "I remember Thee upon my bed and meditate on Thee in the night watches" (Psalm 63:6); again: "Seven times a day do I praise Thee because of Thy righteous judgments" (Psalm 119: 164); and: "As the hart panteth after the water brooks, so panteth my soul after Thee, O God" (Psalm 42:1); or: "My soul thirsteth after Thee, as a thirsty land" (Psalm 143:6). Similarly, patterning our prayer life after that of David, let us ask God for His grace to grow in the art of prayer, for we have the Scriptural assurance that we shall become spiritually the richer for it.

As the Old Testament believers were wont to pray, so also the New Testament Christians, following the example of their Lord and Master, provide us with beautiful models of prayer life.

The New Testament abounds with instances of prayer. In the opening pages of the Gospels are found the songs of praise uttered by Elizabeth and Mary when they meet following the Annunciation. The aged Simeon, holding the infant Savior in his arms, prays. Many suppliants, afflicted in some manner physically or spiritually, fall on their knees and entreat the divine Healer. The Samaritan, cured of his leprosy, is sufficiently grateful to return to thank the Savior. On various occasions before and after the resurrection the masculine and feminine disciples of Christ fall down before Him and worship Him. After the Savior's ascension Stephen prays for his enemies who are stoning him to death. Peter and John pray for the bestowal of the gift of the Holy Spirit upon the believers at Samaria. At the raising of Tabitha from the dead, Peter prays, and again on the housetop of Simon the tanner at Joppa.

But the man who affords all Christians the most admirable pattern of the active prayer life is one who during Jesus' days in the flesh was not a disciple — St. Paul. Saul, the self-confident Pharisee and pupil of the renowned Gamaliel, is on the Damascus road brought to his knees in prayer after that awful vision of Him whom he had been so fiercely persecuting. Together with Barnabas, and then again with Silas, he travels about strengthening the brethren and praying. As Paul and Barnabas lie bound in the prison at Philippi, they pray at the midnight hour. Taking leave of the congregation at Ephesus, Paul kneels in prayer. On board ship bound for Rome in the custody of the centurion Julius, Paul breaks bread and gives thanks. When stranded by shipwreck on the island of Melita, he prays at the bedside of the father of their host Publius, restoring him from fever and flux to health. Even lodged in chains at Rome, particularly during his second imprisonment, when the apostle realizes that his life is of short duration, he prays.

Accordingly, from the time of his conversion to his death at Rome, Paul lived the fruitful prayer life. His epistles are replete with evidence of his prayer activity. Surely, after Paul had learned to pray upon his conversion, he prayed "without ceasing." His prayer life may serve as a guide for all Christians.

It would be impossible to enumerate all the models of prayer life which have been lived during the nineteen centuries following the Savior's death. But a few will suffice to demonstrate that there have been Christians since apostolic times who have led lives of prayer.

A familiar illustration is that of Polycarp, bishop of Smyrna, who, ascending the pyre of martyrdom in his ninetieth year, expired with the praise of God on his lips.

Again, there is the instance of Monica, the mother of Augustine, referred to previously, who for twenty years prayed for the conversion of her brilliant but wicked son.

And from the days of the Reformation we recall the examples of Savonarola and Huss, both of whom — while burning at the stake — prayed for their enemies.

But of that age Luther stands out as the most illustrious example of a hero in prayer. His courage, earnestness, and fervency while engaged in prayer are well known. While at the Coburg he prayed three hours daily. His motto was couched in these familiar words: "To pray diligently is more than half the task." This motto he also reduced to practice, for he declared the busier he was the more he prayed.

Concerning Luther an acquaintance of Valerius Herberger reports, "In prayer his eyes would sparkle and glitter" (California and Nevada District *Proceedings,* 1912, p. 34). Veit Dietrich, once Luther's confidential secretary, described the effect on himself of one of Luther's prayers overheard accidentally: "As I [once] from a distance heard him praying with such [confident] words and clear voice, my heart burned within me for great joy, in that I heard him speaking with God in such friendly and intimate fashion, especially, however, because he advanced promises from the psalms with such positive confidence as if he were certain that what he desired must surely happen." (California and Nevada District *Proceedings,* 1912, pp. 34, 35)

Like Luther, many of his associates in the work of the Reformation learned the art of fervent prayer. For instance, it is related of the priest Johannes Heuglin that when in 1527 he heard the decree read which sentenced him to death by fire, he said: "May God forgive you this sin, for you do not know what you do." Thereupon he prayed: "I thank Thee, eternal God, because Thou hast honored me so highly by permitting me to become a witness of Thy divine truth and hast given me the grace to sacrifice my life for Thy sake." On the way to the place of execution he sang psalms and finally expired in Jesus' name. (*Lutheraner,* 1893, p. 70)

Also, the prominent preacher and hymn writer Christian Scriver (17th century) tells how his pious mother was accustomed each morning to pray for the welfare of her children one after another, especially for the son whom she had consecrated for the ministry while he still lay in his cradle, reminding the Lord that He had promised to be "the Father of the fatherless and a Judge of the widows." Her regularity and fervency of prayer encouraged Scriver to model his prayer life after hers.

Again, as individuals of the Bible pray, so do entire groups and congregations. After Christ's ascension into heaven the disciples come together with one accord to pray. With prayer they select a twelfth apostle to fill the vacancy created by the suicide of Judas. After the Day of Pentecost they remain with one another in prayer. In Acts 4 is recorded the prayer of the congregation at Jerusalem for help and protection against its enemies. This same congregation praises God for reported success of the Gospel among the heathen. As Peter lies chained in prison, the congregation "without ceasing" prays for his release. After his miraculous deliverance from prison Peter finds the congregation assembled in prayer at the house of Mary. The congregation at Antioch prays at the commissioning of Paul and Barnabas for their work among the heathen. And finally, at Tyre the congregation escorts Paul to the gates of the city, kneels, and prays.

Such New Testament examples of united prayer ought to be a powerful incentive for Christian congregations today to unite their hearts and voices in earnest prayer. Surely such collective prayer, because it expresses the fervent plea of a multitude of consecrated hearts, should exert an especially great influence on the Lord of heaven. However, in such prayer fellowship we should be careful to choose as our associates those who are united with us in the true faith, for Paul admonishes (Romans 16:17): "I beseech you, brethren, mark them which cause divisions and offenses contrary to the doctrine which ye have learned, and avoid them." These words of the apostle's warning are, of course, no barrier to prayer fellowship with those of our own persuasion of faith. It is particularly this united prayer of the individual congregation and of the church at large that we should assiduously cultivate for the inestimable benefit of the work in the Lord's kingdom.

Nor should we be blind to the fine examples of prayer life being lived about us in the Church Militant. When our hearts become cold and indifferent, we ought to permit ourselves to be stimulated by the prayers and hymns of our fellow Christians in the public service. Particularly when we are depressed spiritually, we ought to seek the inspiration of common song and prayer to be found within the hallowed precincts of God's house. As we sit in the pews, we should permit our sluggish spirit to be stirred by the pious examples of prayer set by those who sit or stand about us, and we ought to join wholeheartedly in the singing of those powerful hymns of praise such as "Praise to the Lord, the Almighty, the King of Creation," "Now Thank We All Our God," and "Oh, that I Had a Thousand Voices." Then, as the smoking or extinguished brand commences to glow again when ignited by contact with glowing embers, our cold and indifferent spirit will commence to glow once more and commune again in fervent prayer with our God.

Finally, the blessed example of the saints and angels in heaven should move us to prayer. The imperfect life of prayer which the members of the Church Militant have led in the kingdom of grace is now perfectly executed by them as members of the Church Triumphant. According to John the Revelator's vision of heaven, they stand in the presence of the Lamb, clothed in white garments with palms in their hands, and sing, "Blessing and honor and glory and power be unto Him that sitteth upon the throne and unto the Lamb forever and ever." The angels likewise praise the Lord with ceaseless song before His throne, even as the prophet Isaiah so beautifully describes that vision of the hosts of seraphim standing before the Lord and caroling one to another that paean of praise: "Holy, holy, holy is the Lord of hosts; the whole earth is full of His glory."

Could we in spirit transport ourselves to heaven and with glorified eye and ear perceive those perfect models of prayer life, we should return to earth with a new and burning zeal to commune with the Triune God in uninterrupted supplication, thanks, and praise.

XVI

The Advantages

of Family Prayer

FINALLY, a chapter on family devotions, whose rich blessings also should prompt us to pray.

Man has correctly been called a "creature of habit" in the sense that his life to a great extent is governed by the habits he develops. Since good habits will influence him for good, it is not amiss to speak of the establishment of the habit of holding family devotions. In fact, this treatise would not be complete were it to be concluded without reference to this time-honored custom of applying the principles of prayer to everyday life.

For those who have not yet adopted family devotions, a few general recommendations are in order regarding the procedure to be followed in worshiping at the family altar.

The family or home devotions, as the name suggests, are to be devotions. Such they can be only if the Word of God is used. No number of devotional books (and there are many on the market) can ever replace the Bible. Even though such devotional books contain the Word of God, the Bible must be the source and norm of our Christian knowledge and doctrine.

If the family circle is made up entirely of adults, the Bible in a modern translation may readily be used for family devotions. In fact, it is fine if the entire Bible can be read in this manner during the course of time. It probably is not advisable to read all of the books of the Bible in the succession in which they are found. Rather, for the sake of a better survey or perspective of the doctrines of the Bible, it may be well to approach the Scriptures from the viewpoint of fulfillment, reading first the Gospels and then particularly the letters of St. Paul before reading the Old Testament. Or one may proceed by reading an entire book of the New Testament and then shift to some Old Testament book, thus alternating between the Old and the New Testament.

Never, however, should a person read haphazardly in the Scriptures, selecting a chapter here and a chapter there. It is far better to complete the reading of an entire book of the Bible before commencing another, in order to obtain a better picture of the author's purpose in writing the book, of the doctrines contained in the book, and of the context in which familiar or difficult passages occur.

In homes where there are children or adolescents, devotional booklets may be used in addition to the Bible. Many of these are available today, general or seasonal, permanently bound or in paper edition, and they have met with great demand. In fact, devotional booklets have become so popular that a number are published regularly, such as *Portals of Prayer,* a booklet which appears every two months, with timely devotions for each day — each consisting of a suggested Bible reading, a meditation based thereon, and a brief prayer. Either before or afterward, other prayers may be read or spoken, followed by the Lord's Prayer.

Whether a printed or extemporaneous prayer should be used depends on circumstances. Many beautiful prayers appear in prayer and devotional books. However, sometimes an *ex corde* prayer is preferable to comply with a particular need. Where circumstances permit, a song may be sung at the beginning or at the close of the devotions.

Christian parents may also employ the family devotions for a gradual review of the Catechism, to benefit their children. With regard to all these suggestions it should be noted that Scripture makes no definite prescriptions, and consequently these matters are entirely optional.

Several general observations concerning family devotions remain to be made. As to the question "Who shall conduct the devotions?" the general recommendation points to the father, since God has ordained that the father should be the head of the household. If because of sickness or work or for some other compelling reason he is forced to be absent, the mother or one of the children may substitute. If the devotions are held at mealtime, it is advisable to include also the table prayers as part of the devotions.

In families where the children are old enough to read, each member of the family may take his or her turn in reading the devotional material or saying the prayer. For younger children *My Devotions* is an ideal booklet to use. It is published monthly, has realistic pictures, and is adapted to the child level.

The family devotions should be held whenever it is possible to assemble the entire family, whether this be in the morning, in the evening, or at mealtime. Some families hold devotions both in the morning and in the evening. Certainly the oftener they are held the better it will be for all concerned.

Since the home devotions are to be true devotions, they should be neither too long nor too short. There should be nothing to distract the attention of the worshipers. A spirit of peace and quiet should prevail.

Family worship conducted in the spirit of true Christian devotion has the promise of rich spiritual benefits. This meditation on God's Word, coupled with prayer — both integral parts of the home devotions — is conducive to promoting Christian knowledge, to strengthening faith, to growth in holiness of life, and to rich comfort in time of trial.

First of all, meditation on the Word of God will stimulate growth in Christian knowledge. The believer who holds family devotions and ponders on what he reads will thereby impress on his mind and heart the truths which he has learned in catechetical instruction or from sermons, for while he is reading sections from Scripture and expositions of related Bible passages he is familiarizing himself with the context in which these truths were spoken. At the same time he will become acquainted with portions of the Bible not treated in instruction for confirmation and not referred to in the sermon except in isolated instances. Thus it follows that the Christian who participates thoughtfully in the home devotions will gradually become better indoctrinated, and the sermons which he later hears will become more meaningful to him and as a result more interesting. This is a blessing which should not be underestimated.

Meditation in prayer also helps to advance us in Christian knowledge. The knowledge of sin and grace, which can never be divorced from true faith, is a gift of God's Holy Spirit. Daily we should pray for growth in knowledge of God and His works as we do in the First Petition of the Lord's Prayer, "Hallowed be Thy name." The name of God is venerated as holy among Christians when God blesses them with the true and pure possession of His Word and when He in His mercy safeguards them against false doctrine. All believers should pray for growth in Christian knowledge, and God will assuredly answer such prayer. For the divine answer family devotions can be a prominent factor.

The second blessing associated with family devotions is strengthening of faith. Not all persons are equally strong in faith. Some Christians enjoy a firm and vigorous faith, while others are weak and wavering. But even the strongest faith will grow sickly and pale if it is not fed. Spiritual food is the Word of God. Therefore as we daily provide for the nourishment of our mortal bodies, so also should we make provision for the nourishment of our immortal souls. As our bodies grow weak and weary when they are deprived of even one day's supply of food, so also our faith suffers when it is denied even a daily portion of the Bread of Life found in the Gospel. If the Christian does not experience daily hunger for the Word of God, not all is well within. Therefore God's Holy Spirit must daily protect, preserve, and strengthen the faith within our hearts. This He has promised to do through the Gospel which is read in the daily family devotions. Hence the home devotions serve to strengthen our faith.

Not to be disregarded, however, is the fact that the prayers in family devotions also assist in strengthening and preserving faith. Although prayer is no means of grace by which faith is bestowed apart from the Gospel, God has distinctly commanded Christians to pray for spiritual blessings and has promised to answer such prayers. Thus we pray for the growth of our faith each time we speak the Lord's Prayer, particularly in the Second, Third, Sixth, and Seventh Petitions. Since the Lord's Prayer should be used at devotions, it follows that the thoughtful speaking of this prayer of prayers helps to preserve and establish the Christian faith.

A further blessing of family devotions is the help they afford for growth in holiness of life. Every Christian is conscious of his imperfection and readily admits that he daily sins much in ignorance and weakness. But he also realizes that it is God's will that he grow in holiness and abound in love. The agency through which God imparts the willingness and strength to conform to His divine will is once again the Gospel. All of Scripture serves this purpose. The Law helps us spiritually by revealing to us the holy and just will of God and by pointing us to what according to God's standards constitutes truly good works. More than this the Law cannot accomplish. Only the Gospel of the grace of God in Christ Jesus will enable us both to will and to do according to the Lord's good pleasure. This Gospel is, or at least should be, a part of the daily devotions. If it is read diligently, attentively, and meditatively, it must cause us to grow in holiness of life.

Likewise prayer in the family devotions, provided it is not mere lip service, will stimulate the Christian in sanctification. As he daily associates with the Word of God, he realizes more and more his own utter unworthiness and consequent inability to please God. This recognition of the absence of any personal merit will impel him to plead daily with David for divine assistance, saying: "Create in me a clean heart, O God, and renew a right spirit within me" (Psalm 51:10). Assuredly God hears such prayers and in answer to them provides the believer with strength to persevere in good works. Therefore prayer in the family devotions also helps the Christian lead a holy, God-pleasing life.

And yet the life of every Christian here below remains imperfect and is constantly hampered by frailties and imperfections. The reason for this situation lies largely in the believer's sluggishness in prayer. He has not, because he does not ask. Where the Word of God is diligently searched and prayer assiduously cultivated, one may rightfully expect a peaceable and blessed family to flourish. The members of such a household will treat one another with love and respect. They will be a tremendous asset to their congregation; for those who read the Bible most faithfully at home and pray most sincerely are as a rule the most regular attendants at divine worship, partake most frequently of the blessed Sacrament of the Altar, and take the most active part in congregational work. Moreover, all Christians would be far more circumspect in their public conduct as citizens of their country and in their contact with the world if they would commence and close each day with prayer. The influence of daily family prayer in making Christians better citizens is obvious.

Finally, family devotions afford rich comfort in affliction. As long as Christians live on earth they are exposed to crosses and tribulations. This should not appear strange to them, for the Scriptures plainly warn: "We must through much tribulation enter into the kingdom of God" (Acts 14:22). Every Christian individual and every Christian home has its peculiar cross, its measure of suffering appointed by God. Particularly in time of need the blessings of daily home devotions become most manifest. He who in times of prosperity has stocked himself well with comforting Bible passages will not in days of anguish and sorrow be at a loss to find comfort in the treasures of Scripture. If he has been diligent in his study of the holy Volume, he will have committed some passages to memory. Others he will be able to locate with little difficulty. The evident assistance of family devotions in this respect needs no further demonstration.

God also wishes us to pray in times of need, for He has explicitly commanded: "Call upon Me in the day of trouble." Prayer is an art which is learned only in the school of God's Holy Spirit, an art which we must always practice. Family devotions are a laboratory for prayer. There we may daily pour out our hearts before God. There we may plead our needs both great and small. And since our prayer in family devotions is associated with the Scriptures, we learn from the exhortations of the Word of God and from Scriptural models of prayer life that we should worship our heavenly Father in spirit and in truth. Blessed is the Christian who in good times has cultivated the noble art of prayer and who has faithfully conducted family devotions. He will not be caught unawares or unprepared when urgent need brings him to his knees. He looks forward to the end of his earthly pilgrimage with joy, and by storing his mind with the sweet comfort which only God's Word can give he is really preparing himself for that final titanic struggle with death, whose agony will try the

mettle of even the stanchest pilgrim. In the words of
the Christian poet he learns to say:

> When my last hour cometh,
> Fraught with strife and pain,
> When my dust returneth
> To the dust again,
> On Thy truth relying,
> Through that mortal strife,
> Jesus, take me, dying,
> To eternal life.

— James Montgomery

Thus the practice of family devotions produces rich
comfort for the greatest of all trials, death. Therefore
let us not permit this precious, time-honored heirloom —
transmitted to us from godly ancestors — to lapse into
disuse.

In conclusion, although we as sanctified Christians
still suffer from the weakness of our sinful flesh, which
inclines us to be indifferent and lukewarm toward prayer,
God according to His clear Gospel promises will pardon
our spiritual lethargy and will give us the grace of
fervent prayer if only we will repentantly and trustingly
petition Him. Let us therefore enlist the divine aid of
our all-compassionate Savior in the endless battle against
sluggishness in prayer as we plead in the words of the
father of the epileptic child, "Lord, I believe; help Thou
mine unbelief" (Mark 9:24). May we resolve in the
familiar words of Joshua, "As for me and my house,
we will serve the Lord." Then, as truly devout servants
of the Lord, we shall experience the joy of a rich
prayer life.

Lord, teach us to pray

BIBLIOGRAPHY

Bounds, E. M. *Power Through Prayer*. Grand Rapids, Mich.: Zondervan Publishing House.

Buchheimer, L. *From Advent to Advent*. St. Louis, Mo.: Concordia Publishing House.

Burgess and Proudlove. *Watching unto Prayer*. London, England: Lutterworth Press.

California and Nevada District Proceedings, 1912.

Central District Proceedings, 1924.

Christian Century Magazine. March 13, 1935.

Concordia Pulpit, Vol. VII. St. Louis, Mo.: Concordia Publishing House.

Crowell, Grace Noll. *The Lifted Lamp*. New York, N. Y.: Harper & Brothers.

Dietrich. *Catechism.*

Evans, Wm. *Why Pray?* Grand Rapids, Mich.: Wm. Eerdmans Co.

Feucht, Oscar. *The Practice of Prayer*. St. Louis, Mo.: Concordia Publishing House.

Hallesby, O. *Prayer*. Minneapolis, Minn.: Augsburg Publishing House.

Harrison, Norman B. *His Is a Life of Prayer*. Chicago, Ill.: Moody Press.

Hastings, James. *The Christian Doctrine of Prayer*. (Vol. I of *Great Christian Doctrines*.) New York, N. Y.: Charles Scribner and Sons.

Horner, William Wallace. *Let Us Pray*. Montgomery, Ala.: The Paragon Press.

Laubach, Frank C. *Prayer — The Mightiest Force in the World*. New York, N. Y.: Fleming H. Revell.

Luther, Martin. *A Short Explanation of Dr. Martin Luther's Small Catechism*. St. Louis, Mo.: Concordia Publishing House.

Lutheraner, 1893.

Luther's Works. Erlangen edition.

Luther's Works. St. Louis edition.

Luther's Works. Weimar edition.

Macartney, Clarence E. *Prayer — At the Golden Altar*. New York, N. Y.: Fleming H. Revell.

Mackenzie, W. Douglas. *Pater Noster Sheen; or, Light on Man's Destiny*. New York, N. Y.: Harper & Bros.

Maier, Walter A. *Winged Words for Christ*. St. Louis, Mo.: Concordia Publishing House.

Mueller, J. T. *Christian Dogmatics*. St. Louis, Mo.: Concordia Publishing House.

Murray, Andrew. *The Prayer Life*. Grand Rapids, Mich.: Zondervan Publishing House.

Nicholson, Martha Snell. "Prayer for the Home." Chicago, Ill.: Moody Press.

Nicoll, W. Robertson. *Prayer in War Time*. New York, N. Y.: George Doran.

Pieper, Franz. *Christliche Dogmatik*. St. Louis, Mo.: Concordia Publishing House.

Proctor, William. *The Principles and Practice of Prayer*. London, England: Oliphants.

Robertson, Ella Broadus. *Along the Highway of Prayer*. Grand Rapids, Mich.: Zondervan Publishing House.

Sabiers, Karl. *The Prayer Life*. Los Angeles, Calif.: Robertson Publishing Co.

Talling, M. P. *Extempore Prayer*. New York, N. Y.: Fleming H. Revell.

Zwemer, Samuel M. *Taking Hold of God*. Grand Rapids, Mich.: Zondervan Publishing House.